Measuring performance in human service systems

James F. Budde

Measuring performance in human service systems

Planning, organization, and control

amacom

A division of American Management Associations

Library of Congress Cataloging in Publication Data

Budde, James F
  Measuring performance in human service systems.

  Bibliography: p.
  Includes index.
  1. Management. 2. Social work administration.
  I.   Title.
HD31.B76947   658.4   79-19551
ISBN 0-8144-5551-4

First Printing

To Chip and Anne,
for their energies and idealism;

to Jane,
for her patience and understanding;

and to other loved ones,
for their wisdom and spirit.

Preface

When we were younger and more naive, many of us were awed by the prestige and mystique of the "boss's office." We imagined great decisions being made with absolute authority by an infallible mental giant behind the gold-lettered door. Too often we fantasized the manager as a handsome, well-dressed gentleman in a dark-blue suit who drove a white Lincoln convertible and spent his abundant leisure time at the country club. The Top Man was endowed with money, prestige, and power. "It ain't all that way, friends," as many of us have found out. There are numerous complex problems that plague the manager and require major expenditures of time. But there is no absolute authority to solve those problems, and leisure activities are often only a figment of the imagination because many weekends are spent in the office catching up on the workload.

Behind the once-mystifying, awe-inspiring office door are ringing phones and blinking lights signifying an array of callers. Within the office are stacks on stacks of papers, all representing complex problems. Many papers are filed away, but others are piled on the floor. There's also a pile of letters and memos, each about a special problem. In particular is that one from "the big boss." And outside the office there's a line of people waiting to see the manager, each with a special problem.

What thoughts has the infallible administrator on his mind? He may be preoccupied with an upcoming meeting with the big boss. He could well be concerned with the unrest of certain emancipated women employees or perhaps even the floating crap game in one of his departments. It's likely there is some conflict among several staff members over some trivial issue. There is probably a budget that has been overspent, and there may be no funds to make up the deficit. He may even have paranoid questions: "What does my staff think of me?" "What is going to happen to this organization?" "What will I do when he quits?" One of the biggest concerns might be "What are they doing now?" "Are they working as hard as they should be?" "Had I better check those time cards?" Or perhaps even "Why don't they leave me alone!"

To be sure, the preceding examples are somewhat extreme, but they do reflect the day-to-day realities. Management is no bed of roses—it requires a unique set of skills and interests. Not everyone can or should be a manager. As Laurence J. Peter has said, too often staff are promoted to their highest level of incompetence. On the other hand, there are those who enjoy management and have developed or acquired the skills necessary to manage an organization effectively and economically.

This book was developed specifically for the administrator who chooses to acquire knowledge and skills that will lead to effective management. In particular, it was written for administrators of human services— schools, prisons, welfare agencies, employment agencies, medical service organizations, mental health institutions, community mental retardation agencies, and the like. The content, however, is applicable to managers in business and industry at all levels.

In management there will always be problems; but when an organization is plagued with so many problems that it cannot perform appropriately, the situation becomes intolerable. If the organization then survives, it will have limited impact. Sound management practices implemented with skill and the appropriate tools can minimize the number of organizational problems. In order to minimize problems, certain difficulties must be eliminated; but better than eliminating them is not allowing them to occur. People cause most problems; therefore, the trick is to manage individuals in such a way that they do not cause problems but instead perform at levels compatible with the organization's objectives.

Measuring Performance in Human Service Systems was not meant as a guide to solving incidental problems. Enough about those problems! Here's what this book is really about: (1) providing organizational direction, (2) specifying organizational performance standards, and (3) so managing employees that performance standards are met. Too often in human services direction, performance is merely a concept. Everyone seems to have a different idea about where the organization is going and whether it is getting there. Lack of congruent criteria is a major problem in human service and a source of recurrent concerns. In this text, the author provides a general management model and numerous examples of cases and tools that are used to specify direction and evaluate performance. Examples in this book, if followed, can enable a manager to acquire objective information about his organization so he can make sound decisions and manage staff effectively.* This book illustrates how the process is used to improve both the organization and the individuals within it. It is written so the individual manager can develop his unique management model by drawing from the general model and overall content.

Measuring Performance in Human Service Systems may not help you solve the dilemma of the floating crap game, but it should help you to improve the job performance of those who are playing it. When you think about it, good job performance is no minor accomplishment. At the very least, when performance is high and the organization is running smoothly, the manager has time to attend to other potentially touchy situations. But there is something more: a certain pride in making the organization do what it is supposed to do and do it well. Without a doubt, high performance is the result of all employees' work, but it is attributable to sound management practices. So we have provided you with a general management model for a number of management procedures and related tools, plus occasional reminders that humor also has its place in the system.

One final word. Books are never created in a vacuum, and this one is no exception. My most sincere thanks to Barbara McLean and our colleagues at Project MORE who edited and pulled together the final manuscript.

James F. Budde

* It goes without saying that a manager may be of either gender and that neither administrative difficulties nor the capacities to overcome them are peculiar to the one or the other. But English is lacking in acceptable neutral pronouns, so the masculine ones are used to avoid the clumsiness of "he or she" and "his or her."

Contents

Measuring performance in human service systems

1

Managing performance: the job and the world around you

"Johnny is smoking in the restroom?" "They are making Affirmative Action charges against me?" "You mean you still haven't received your paycheck?" "She hasn't received any services?" "The federal government is requiring what?" "My staff member did what?" "What do they mean we have made no impact?" As an administrator, you are well aware of similar crises and more. As one administrator complained recently, "It isn't fun being an administrator any more." The management process has certainly become more complex and will undoubtedly continue to grow in complexity. Administrators, if they are to be effective managers, will need to use the best means available to solve the problems that have plagued, and will continue to plague, human services. Functional management principles, strategies, tools, and procedures that provide solutions for human service managers is what this book is all about.

1

Where We Have Been and Where We Are Going

Before taking a look at principles, strategies, and so on, let us take a look at where human services are today and where they are going. Some attention should be paid to the general social framework that surrounds human services in order to comprehend the origin of the general conditions that affect the day-to-day work of a manager.

We live in a capitalist society. It was developed around the concept of the free enterprise system: anyone could go into any business that he liked and try to earn a living at it. Usually, if an individual had chosen a fairly good business, the harder he worked the more money he would make. The process had natural reward value, and typically the cycle of harder work and financial rewards spiraled. In the beginning, there were few social services or governmental controls, two major factors in society today. The boss spent most of his time providing goods and/or services. When the goods or services did not meet the consumer's needs in a competitive market, business would drop off. There was a natural attrition of poor businesses.

Over time there were injustices, so government intervened. Governmental controls were developed to protect consumers from poor and unethical business practices. Labor unions were formed to protect employees. The economy swelled to the point where it could afford more and more social programs to aid the poor, the handicapped, the unemployed, and the uneducated.

What has happened today? For everyone's good, monstrous federal programs and "controls" have been developed. It is sometimes questionable how much they control or accomplish, other than requiring huge amounts of paperwork. It is also questionable how effective the social programs are. There are strong labor unions whose avarice has been known to cause businesses to fail or whose acts have created severe hardships for the entire country. There are businesses that will cut sharp corners to make a profit. Most major businesses have strong lobbies in Washington. When a business is in trouble, the lobbies bring strong pressure to eliminate controls or acquire funds for an unprofitable industry that would and perhaps should go broke. That, of course, averts natural attrition.

Where have all of the businesses that finance this country gone? In 1974 Drucker stated that "more than half the gross national product goes to or through service institutions that are not a business and are not held accountable for economic performance nor subject to market tests." That ratio is even higher today. Without accountability for economic performance of some kind, the contribution that these services make to the economy of the country is highly questionable. It must be noted, however, that most human services were not developed to make profits. They were developed to meet the needs of certain people and were financed by government. That has produced an interesting phenomenon. Not only is there no valid accountability for economics, which is not totally justifiable, but there is little accountability for programs or services, which is certainly justifiable. If present trends continue, there will be growth in human services and there will be little emphasis on economic or program accountability—that is, until the limit of public support is reached. Indicators for the first time suggest that the public may be reaching the limit.

Having an independent business, even a small one, carries less glamor and prestige than in the past. Perhaps entrepreneurs have found better opportunities in service institutions or government, where there is little account-ability and life is easier. And what about all the social programs? They have been growing by leaps and bounds. What is wrong with that? Nothing, if the country can afford them and if they are effective in meeting the needs of the consumers they are to serve.

What conclusions can a manager draw from the present state of affairs? First, let's postulate some general predictions:

- There will continue to be more monies for social programs, although the popularity of the programs is declining.
- Inflation will continue to provide more dollar payment as the GNP business dollar shrinks.
- As social programs increase, and as a result of misuse of funds and injustice to civil and human rights, the bureaucracy will increase in size and scope in order to implement and control social programs. More control will be required by state government.
- Big business will continue to grow and develop and improve its technology, although the rate could decline.
- Labor unions will continue to grow in human service areas.
- More and more energy and resources will be used to deal with industry, labor unions, government, and consumer rights.

Some specific predictions are the following:

1. Human service managers will be provided with opportunities for new and additional sources of revenue

for human services. The increases will not be as dramatic as those seen in the last few years.

2. Because of continued inflation, pay increases for employers and managers will have less and less incentive value. Human services will cost more to operate, and the pool of highly qualified workers will be small.

3. Over the past several decades, the amount of paperwork and management time needed to comply with federal and state regulations has grown enormously. It will continue to grow, and more specialized manpower will be required to deal with government regulations and requirements. Effectiveness will vary, but the regulations should provide some overall improvement in human services. Cost-effectiveness of regulations will be questionable in a number of instances.

4. As business grows, additional technology that can be used to improve human services and the management of human services will be developed. In fact, human services now provide a large marketplace for some businesses. Universities and a new breed of students will continue to contribute to the implementation of the technology. Managers will need to develop understanding and skills to use the new technologies. In some instances, new special staff will be needed or trained to make use of the technology. There will be no major or rapid assimilation of the technology.

5. Because of unresolvable complications in employees' lives, labor unions will gain more favor. Already human service personnel who once thought it unethical to join a union have become strong supporters. Administrators will therefore need to develop additional skills, spend additional time and effort, and/or acquire additional specialized staff to deal with union actions.

6. Support services and personnel needed to deal with technological advances, labor union bargaining, government regulations, and consumer rights will grow in order to counterbalance the thrusts in those areas. Actual services to the consumer will probably not grow accordingly, and in some cases they could be impeded by growth in the above areas. It is quite possible that somewhat less attention will be directed to services and there will be less accountability because energies are redirected to other areas.

Although the trends and conclusions are not complete and are not entirely true of or applicable to each manager's situation, they are pertinent to the current state of affairs. It is not our intent to pass judgment on the necessity for that state of affairs or to try to determine if the nation is better off with its intricate complexities than with its past injustices. It should be noted, however, that many of its citizens are highly frustrated not only with some of the old problems but with the human services solutions.

From a manager's standpoint, old problems as well as the rapid changes and new trends must be dealt with as they are laid on the doorstep. Perhaps the biggest problems are recognizing change as opportunity and dealing with it. So should one get out of management and "join the ranks"? *Certainly not!* Dealing with change has always been a major aspect of administration and certainly management. It will continue to be a major aspect, one with increasing impact.

Some of the old roles of managers are questionable and others remain sound. One must capitalize on that which works and integrate it with what is needed. In a new type of ball game, an administrator does not always know what is needed. Finding what works—effectively and economically—is really the management process. After all, if there were no problems that needed solutions, who would need an administrator or manager?

What Are Human Services and Human Service Systems?

"Human services" are defined, for this text, as being assistance to a target group that is aimed at eliminating or reducing a social problem. Emphasis is typically placed on meeting the needs and improving the lifestyles of the individuals who receive the services. Human services can be private or public, profit or nonprofit, and purchasable by a third party or by the consumer. Some typical examples are education, social welfare, medicine, vocational rehabilitation, corrections, and mental health. The term "human service system" is used to describe the overall complex network of human services and the processes by which they are provided. This includes financing and administration and support systems, as well as the services and the consumers.

The Manager and Performance Management

Who should be concerned about the performance of human services when there are so many other problems? Everyone who has an interest in the welfare of this nation, and for some very good reasons.

First of all, there is the serious question just how much the nation *can* afford to spend for human services. If the revenues from business that are used to finance human services continue to shrink, if inflation continues to rise, and if more specialized human services personnel are required to deal with red tape, there will be less money for the human services end. If management within human services cannot maximize the quality, quantity, and efficiency of human services, the dollars required to operate the services will undoubtedly continue to increase. The byproduct, of course, will be inefficiency and poorer services.

As crises arise from poor service, and they certainly will arise, the typical solution as in the past will be requests for more and more dollars to improve the services. The problem is that there is a bottom in the barrel and it is quite possible that dollars will not always be available to bail human services out of crises. In fact, we could well be approaching the bottom of the barrel. The management of performance within human services is a critical factor in developing and maintaining the quality, quantity, and efficiency of human services.

The second reason for concern has less to do with efficiency than with the quality and quantity of human services. Crises brought on by poor services and mismanagement eventually arouse the public. The legislative branch of government then gets involved and takes action, usually one resulting in intervention. The process of implementing the intervention is then passed on to the appropriate agency. Eventually, the administration of the human services is faced with complying with regulations or standards that were intended to eliminate poor services and abuses. That means more work for the organization and the use of additional resources to comply with standards or regulations that might have only a minimal effect on eradicating the original problems. Note that the management of performance within the organization from the beginning could have gone a long way toward avoiding any intervention at all. It is possible that tools and techniques that could have been used by management in the beginning would have been less costly and more effective than those imposed.

The nursing home industry is a good example of the problem. In recent years, there has been a good deal of evidence of poor performance, mismanagement, and outright crime. Not all nursing homes were guilty, of course, but the problems were rather widespread. In due course there was public outrage and legislative action, and now there is government intervention. Standards have been set, and federal and state governments have invested large sums for the staff and resources needed to implement them. Some states and organizations are fighting them. Some parts of the standards are being questioned because of omissions, irrelevancies, and overall effects. Nevertheless, the standards will be implemented and they will effect some improvement of services. And who suffers? The taxpayer, the administrator, and possibly even the consumer who is entitled to good services.

The third reason for concern is the degree of accountability that is being brought about. In addition to the traditional investigative agents, numerous new agents, such as those concerned with human and civil rights protection and advocacy and environmental protection, must be dealt with by the human services administrator. To be sure, some of the laws and agents have aided in protecting the taxpayer and the consumer. But they have also served to open the door to unnecessary audits, investigations, and mediations. If an administrator has not been fair and/or if he cannot demonstrate why certain decisions were made and actions taken, his position is in jeopardy. Accurate data on individuals' performances and accurate performance data on the organization itself will go a long way toward providing the objective information the manager needs to strengthen his position in such matters.

Take the example of the inept administrator who informs an employee that he is performing well when actually he is not. The administrator probably has not specified what the performance should be or evaluated the actual one, and he may not want to bother with such tasks. Inevitably, however, he will become fed up and terminate the low-performing employee. When the employee brings up a grievance or appeals to one of the various agencies, the administrator will be in trouble. Not only will he have mismanaged the employee but he will have insufficient proof of grounds for termination. That puts not only the administrator but the organization as well in a dangerous position. Repetition of such an incident could eventually cost the administrator his job, and justifiably so. As a fellow administrator once said; "The job you save may be your own."

A fourth reason for concern about the performance of a human service organization is the administrator himself. His reputation and career are based on the performance of his organization. Now, everyone knows that it is possible to develop an easy career in public service— or big business, for that matter—by just sitting back and not making waves. Time and rank will slowly move an administrator along the line. But what about that administrator who does just enough to get by? What about the one who dwells on keeping the desks clean and punching the time clock as opposed to achieving high service performance? Certainly in question is how satisfied such individuals are with their jobs and lives and where they are *really* going. Also in question is how others feel about such administrators, what kinds of interactions others have with them, and whether there is not an eventual day of reckoning.

To be sure, an administrator or manager who pushes his organization to perform at too great a rate can find himself in hot water. That is especially true if the administrator does not understand the workings of the organization or what good organizational performance is and how it can be achieved. On the other hand, one who does understand those things and can make them work for him can do much to develop a smooth-running organization, one that meets consumer needs and has high morale. That administrator will reap the benefits.

What Is Human Service Performance?

Human service system performance can be determined only if there are some criteria with which to compare action and accomplishments. Basically, there are two categories of performance with which a manager must be concerned; they are *cost performance* and *program performance*.

Why must administrators of human services be concerned about cost and program performance? They are almost always responsible and accountable for both, and if the administrator is to manage an organization effectively, he must deal with both. The higher emphasis is usually placed on cost performance; there is an authority who commands, "Stay within the budget. Try to spend all of it, but don't spend any more." Less emphasis is placed on program performance, which is more difficult to measure. Here the authority commands, "Provide quality services for all consumers regardless of the resources."

Decisions on the part of the administrator related to cost and program performance directly affect the outcome of the human service. An administrator must therefore be able to determine what cost and program performance are, know how to evaluate them, and know how to manage them. Performance is determined by (1) specifying dimensions for individual performance units, (2) specifying performance standards, that is, the number of units, (3) collecting performance data related to the number of units spent or provided, and (4) comparing the actual performance to performance standards. The results can then be used as a basis for decision making. Also, standards and performance can be adjusted according to need. The process will be covered in detail in Chapter 2.

Cost performance

Cost performance is the actual spending or saving of dollars as determined by a performance standard. It is the easiest performance for an administrator to define and deal with. The reasons are that, first, the dollar can be used as a standard unit. As Anthony states:

> In accounting, a record is made only of those facts that can be expressed in monetary terms. The advantage of expressing facts in monetary terms is that money provides a common denominator by means of which heterogeneous facts about a business can be expressed in terms of numbers that can be added or subtracted.

Second, because cost accountability has had such a high priority over the years, accounting systems have been developed and implemented to record cost data. Although they do not always provide the cost accounting information needed, they do serve as a reliable data source, one that is fairly stable in most human services.

Program performance

Program performance is not as easily defined as cost performance. It may be related, as individual performance is related, to behavior: Johnny is smoking in the restroom; Mary received an A. But which behavior is "good" or "bad" cannot be determined unless it is judged by a predetermined standard. Smoking in restrooms is typically considered bad, and A's are typically considered good. Similarly, good or bad performance of a program cannot be determined unless it is compared with some standard such as ten routine diagnostic units per day. More is good; less is bad.

Evaluating the overall behavior of Johnny is more complex; it comprises numerous behaviors which are compared with overall performance standards. Johnny smoked in the restroom, but he received an A in spelling and math. Similarly, human services comprise numerous behaviors, and the frequencies with which the behaviors occur may be compared with overall performance standards. Ten routine diagnostic units, 20 treatment units, one performance report per day is the standard.

At this point, it should suffice to describe program performance as *organizational behavior that is identifiable and measurable and can be compared with a performance standard.* There are virtually no common program units, such as dollar units, that can be used to define and measure human service programs. But one thing is certain: program performance in human services can be measured, and there are effective means for developing program performance measures.

Performance standards

Performance standards are the criteria against which actual performance is measured. Davis and Behan state that, in some cases, performance measures are implicit in the statement of performance criteria. In other cases the standards are definite points on a scale. Banghart describes the process by which performance standards can be developed:

> The standards might be derived from within or outside the system. One might wish to develop a standard of current operating efficiency and compare a new system with the current standard. Frequently, it will be necessary to utilize standards from without the system and bring the system up to the level of outside standards.

When an organization or system is new or it has not previously been defined with any precision, it is difficult to develop precise performance standards. Banghart wisely states:

> Throughout the systems study the assumption is made that the original objectives have been clearly and concisely stipulated. Often much groundwork is needed before it is possible to determine clear-cut statements of objectives.

Banghart also raises an important point related to performance standards, that of effectiveness:

An evaluation of performance is done in terms of effectiveness. The design of the problem solution determines how effective the new system will be in fulfilling the organization's missions. It is necessary to devise standards for measuring effectiveness.

Usually if a human service program is effective, it is considered to be a good program. Most managers strive to develop and maintain effective programs. Again it should be noted that the effectiveness of human services is often in question and that most administrators have a difficult time validating effectiveness. The reason, of course, is that performance has been neither determined nor measured against performance standards.

Relationship Between Program and Cost Performance

In human services the relation between program and cost performance is rarely considered. The techniques developed to study the relation in other disciplines—cost-benefit and cost-effectiveness—are rarely used in human services. Several years ago, when it was in vogue to use them, such terms as cost-effectiveness were tossed around freely. Administrators implied that their services were cost-effective and filled their proposals for grants with the jargon. Sad to say, however, the trend turned out to be only a fad.

Often there is a direct relation between cost and program performance. A change in one area of performance usually has an effect on another. For example, if there is a cut in funds for staff, the loss of staff could limit the quality of service and impede program performance. On the other hand, if through improvement in program performance funds were saved, cost performance would also be improved. Effects of any changes in performance are critically important to a manager. When he makes key decisions, or even when he routes decisions affecting one category, the manager needs to know the probable effect on the other category. In essence, he must attempt to find the optimum blend.

Most often, human service budgets are increased or decreased in response to political or popular wishes. The frequent results are haphazard financing and too little consideration of program performance, both of which lead to major critical problems within the human service system. The problems of budgeting in human services, without consideration of the direct relation between cost and performance, can become quite complex. They might be compared with those of a family's food budget. A family can, of course, spend too much for groceries; but if its budget is cut too low or eliminated completely, it can starve. Conversely, if too much money is spent, waste can result. Ideally, the family will establish its priorities and determine the components and cost of a healthy diet. From that minimal point, diet and cost can be expanded and substitutions made to determine what may be spent for additional more highly nutritious or appetizing items. As costs change, or as new foods become available, the family must reassess the problem. The dynamics of food and cost must be assessed continually.

What effect do traditional cost increases and decreases have on the performance of human service organizations? The question is often more easily answered by human service organizations that operate for profit, yet the effect of the relation between cost changes and corresponding program performance changes still is often difficult to determine with traditional techniques. The inherent problem is the establishment of the program performance and cost performance relation, so that those who control the purse strings understand the impact of cost manipulation and budget in accordance with program needs. Such actions as an arbitrary 20 percent across-the-board cut should be considered poor management.

It is sad but true that the majority of decisions concerning funding are most often made without any good cost-effectiveness information. Instead such decisions have been influenced by political blackmail, special interest groups, pressure, bureaucratic punishment, and plain old greed. In other cases, they have been based on the most funds at the best matching cost or on a notion that an overall economic cleanup is needed. Why do such practices prevail? If no cost-effectiveness information is available in the sector where decisions concerning funding of human services are made, the way is open to poor and unethical decisions. That is true not only at the top levels of government but also at the level where the services to the consumer are provided. In most instances, those who provide or utilize funds for human services would appropriate or allocate the funds wisely if they had good information on which to base their decisions. Often they scurry around trying and failing to find the information. As a result, they have an incomplete defense against poor management or unethical practices. This is not to say that good data will solve the problem, but it could prove to be an invaluable resource.

Program performance measures must be considered as important as cost performance measures in human service organizations, yet that is an area with which human service administrators are least equipped to deal. If no reliable performance measurements are available, human service administrators must be cautious with respect to the nature and frequency of an organization's performance evaluations. Also, when making decisions, they must be suspicious of the relevance and scope of the data obtained by incomplete measurement procedures.

Conceptual and Technical Reference for Managing Performance

Those who have been responsible for managing others have been concerned about how to do so, and they have developed certain concepts, tools, and techniques to aid them with the process. For example, one of them, Han Fei Tzu, during the third century B.C. in China, explained the concept of performance management in a simple and concise form that remains applicable today:

> The intelligent ruler unifies measures and weights, sets up different standards, and steadfastly maintains them. Therefore, his decrees are promulgated and the people follow them. Laws are models for the empire and the representative standard of affairs . . . .
>
> When a subject makes claims, the ruler gives him work according to what he claimed, but holds him wholly responsible for accomplishment corresponding to this work. When the accomplishment corresponds to the work and the work corresponds to what the man claimed he could do, he is rewarded.

Today, as then, intelligent administrators attempt to develop weights, measures, and standards. Employees are given work. When their accomplishments correspond to the standards, they are rewarded. As a management concept, Han Fei Tzu's statement serves as the ideal to work from. The concept should be adhered to as closely as possible. This is not a simple matter, however, as an intelligent manager will tell you. In today's complex world it is difficult to set standards, direct staff, and reward staff. Initially, because of the background and training of most human service managers, the complexities of human services, and the diverse pressures affecting the manager, too little work of good quality to develop performance standards is done.

The reward process also presents some major difficulties. Even if proof of performance were provided, it is almost impossible to use existing systems to "reward" an employee. Incentives need to be great enough and timely enough to be effective. Existing accounting and personnel systems in human services do not provide effective or timely incentives.

Outside influences from various unions and associations demanding differing standards and rates affect the allocation and amount. Even the action of the state and federal government regarding taxes, efficiency tactics, and wage controls affect the reward structure.

Today's world contains numerous control systems that lump individuals together for purposes of expediency. Yet ironically the emphasis in services is typically on the unique needs of the individual client. What will benefit, motivate, or improve the individual is advocated. Far too often it is assumed that the yearly standard raise, the periodic promotion, the occasional glad hand, the privilege of working for the "Mother Company" are adequate rewards for the *individual* employee in order to maintain high performance. These are bad assumptions.

A Unique Performance Management Model

Management would be an easy task if there were one specific model that would fit every manager's and every organization's needs. Then it might even be possible to use a computer or develop a robot to do the management work; an organization could have its own C3PO or R2D2. The problem is that no two managers or service organizations are the same. Some are similar, and in those instances similar models can be used. Generally, however, every organization will require a unique management model. Development of unique management models depends upon boundaries, needs, constraints, personalities, values, and opportunities within and around a human service system. All those variables change with time. A manager's unique management model should be neither simple nor nebulous; it should have identifiable, measurable components with related timelines, sequences, and flow.

The human service system, like the world around it, is ever-changing. That compels a manager to constantly modify his individual management model. The content depends upon two major factors. First, the content for each management model depends somewhat upon the type of human service (educational, correctional, mental health, or other). Second, each management model is affected over time by numerous variables including (1) the degree and type of accountability, (2) degree of authority delegated, (3) philosophy of the time, (4) mission of the parent organization, (5) size of the unit to be managed, (6) availability of resources, (7) interference by or assistance of crosscutting support services, and (8) the personalities of the staff. What the manager must do is look at the boundaries, constraints, and opportunities of the time and develop a functional management system that gets the job done. If he is to do so, he must pull together into his management model various principles, strategies, tools, procedures, and solutions that are effective for that particular service, situation, and time.

A General Performance Management Model

Numerous management models have been developed by various authorities. For purposes of this text, however, a simple model has been developed to illustrate the key functions involved in the management of performance. The functions can be applied to various types of human service systems as well as to major individual services or support services. The model was designed for comprehensive management application. In order for the individual manager to develop and/or improve his unique management model, the general model can be used as a reference. The general model, in addition to changes and influences in and around the human service system, should be considered when the unique management model is developed and modified. Detailed components and the structure to be included within the unique management model can be developed from content found in the following chapters. It is recommended that the individual manager, with the general model as a reference, use the components that will be described and illustrated for inclusion in the unique model as needed.

Individual management models should be developed and analyzed on a planned formal basis every three to six months. A year is often too long. Of course, when specific problems in certain areas arise, specific or single components can be analyzed and modified to meet them. Once the model is developed and tested, however, changes will be minimal.

The general model, Figure 1-1, consists of two major components: preparation and direction. Preparation is generally concerned with the determination of needs, the planning of work, and the development of performance standards. Direction is generally concerned with implementation and operation of services, evaluation of performance, and maintenance of performance.

The technical base for management of performance in human services has been provided by developments in numerous fields by various individuals. Although this section will not touch on them, it will discuss the general activities within the various functions of the general management model, Figure 1-1.

Determining consumer need

The initial function is to determine just what the consumers of human services need and the general methods

Figure I-I. General management model.

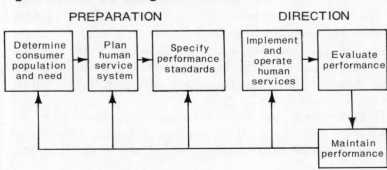

of meeting the needs. The process should begin with a realistic and fresh look. What the consumers actually need is not necessarily what they or the public at large think their needs are or what the human service system has traditionally seen their needs to be. The determination calls for a combination of imagination and creativity coupled with a look at the real world. It also calls for the combining of general need with more effective, economical, and humanistic methods of developing services that meet need. Finally, the function requires taking a look at the market to determine feasibility.

The needs function is critical for the development of the performance standards that will follow; it will provide the overall direction of the system. It is tragic that so little emphasis is placed on it in human services.

Planning the service system

Planning of some sort or the other is used by all managers, but the effort expended, the kinds of tools and procedures used, and the preplanning information developed vary considerably. As a result, plans that are developed differ greatly in utility, quality, and quantity. There are numerous variables that can lead to the provision of inadequate service, and poor planning is certainly one of them. Since the manager cannot control many of the variables, it is essential that he focus on the planning function, over which he usually has a good bit of control.

A major problem in the planning of human services is the assumed complexity of the services. Putting a man on the moon was a complex undertaking. The process used to carry it out was, qualitatively, the same one that the manager must use. It consists in identifying the major components and breaking them down into smaller components that can be comprehended and managed. Sequencing of the components in an orderly fashion that leads to the achievement of objectives or provision of a human product must be integral. Techniques found in systems technology are highly applicable to such purposes.

One additional activity that can be used in planning and is seldom used in human services is simulation. Managers in human services could improve that activity by following the example of Thomas Edison. Edison established the first industrial research laboratory. In order to determine what performance should be and how to control it, procedures were first tested in the laboratory. The work of the laboratory was concerned not only with a task or product but with management control of multiple tasks and products. In short, research was used as the basis for the development and organization of business.

Although that approach is now followed closely in most large businesses, human service allegiance to research and development is only cursory because R&D is viewed as luxurious and overly academic. Short-range programs, the performance and impact of which are seldom determined, are often substituted for research and development that might lead to the improvement of performance in human services. It is tragic that more human service managers do not use this preparatory approach. Even when the approach is followed only to the point of simulation on paper, it can yield invaluable results.

Developing performance standards

Developing performance standards is usually a part of preparatory planning, but it is actually a never-ending process. Standards will need to be adjusted as various variables affect the human services. Fine tuning performance standards, the second step, is not as much of a problem as specifying what the performance standards are to be initially. Fredrick Taylor, the father of scientific management, was one of the first to establish performance rates or standards. One of his initial works, "A Price System Rate," dealt with performance standards and also with managerial efficiency. It is interesting to note that Taylor's objective was to relieve the worker's heavy toil and create a higher standard of living for the worker through increased performance. That was in 1895.

Recent and popular contributions to performance standards can be found in behavioral psychology. Behaviorists have chosen to identify an observable individual behavior and measure the frequency of that behavior. The advantage of this type of measurement is that it is not subject to one sample in time, but total performance is recorded *over time*, in which the subject's behavior increases, decreases, or remains constant. The original work of the behaviorists is attributed to Pavlov in Russia, and to Watson and Thorndike in the United States. B. F. Skinner is typically credited with measuring rate of behavior and also with establishing and standardizing basic principles for changing behavior.

What the behaviorists contributed to the measurement of performance in human services was the technology for developing unit measures and a measurement process. In industry, an end product such as a hairdryer, TV, or automobile can be easily measured as to quality and quantity by developing specifications and comparing quality and quantity with the specifications. In human services the product, whether a change in behavior of a client or the precise behavior of the service provider, was *thought* to be too difficult to measure. By specifying quantity and quality of the behavior desired, however, it is possible to develop performance units which can be compared with a standard and quantified.

Behavioral or performance units can be specified through the use of measurable objectives. Objectives containing behavioral criteria can be used as the basis for evaluating performance and performance standards. An individual's performance is compared with the objectives' measurable criteria, and performance is evaluated as substandard, standard, or above standard.

One basic problem in human services related to the use of behavioral objectives has been the haphazard development of overall systems in which the objectives have been structured. Sequences of objectives that are related and lead to an end product, as covered in planning the service system, are a necessity. Business, industry, and the military have been the leaders in this area. With the rapid growth of large business, the leaders that have emerged have found methods of establishing related objectives at various levels of management. It would probably not surprise the reader that the early leaders were companies like General Motors, Du Pont, and Sears Roebuck. As indicated by Han Fei Tzu, power must be dispersed and performance controlled if a manager is to manage a large organization. But that is also true of a manager who will manage only a few people.

In short, when a manager has completed the three major functions within Preparation, Figure 1-1, there should be a set of measurement units to define numerous service behaviors or products. The service products, because they are standard units, can be quantified and compared with performance standards. Both the product specifications and the performance standards will be included within measurable objectives. Measurable objectives will be structured in an orderly system that will lead to the functional attainment of the overall mission of the human service system, that of meeting consumer needs.

Implementing and operating human services

The first function under Direction, Figure 1-1, is the implementation and operation of the human services. At this point the initial part of the management work is completed and, if it has been done well, the manager theoretically merely says,"go."

In the planning process covered previously, attention was given to planning in general. It should be noted that plans for both implementation and operation need to be developed.

Implementation of human services is a matter of setting up the services. Basically, it involves (1) determining start-up tasks, the details involved for each task, and the available resources and manpower and (2) scheduling resources, manpower, and often budgeting and spending.

In the 1800s Henry Gantt developed a planning, scheduling, and implementation tool that is now called the Gantt chart. Procedures developed by him are particularly applicable today. His work was a direct antecedent of the sophisticated program evaluation and review techniques (PERT) and critical path method (CPM).

Performance evaluation

Evaluation of performance, as discussed earlier, is not a recent development. The major problem with evaluation is that, when the preceding steps are not taken, there are neither data for making an evaluation nor criteria to compare it with. There are numerous techniques that can be used for evaluation once standards are specified and performance data are collected.

Techniques for evaluation covered in this text are basically related to simple frequency measurements. The general tool used will be the frequency chart, on which performance data are plotted and compared with standards. Trends and other characteristics can be evaluated as well. In addition, a standard frequency celeration chart developed by Ogden R. Lindsley will be introduced. The utility of this chart lies in its use to measure a wide range of frequencies.

From the author's viewpoint, evaluation information should be developed and illustrated in a way that is simple and to the point. Appropriateness and usefulness are the main considerations. An administrator seldom needs 100 pages of computer printout or fine statistical analysis.

As noted, evaluating the relation of cost performance and program performance is also a part of evaluation. Again, this is no recent development. Progress in developing the organizational program/cost performance relation was made in the nineteenth century by Henry Towne in his *The Engineer as Economist*. Towne questioned the roles of effectiveness and efficiency in organizations, and he thereby differentiated two concepts that are directly related to cost and performance.

Maintaining performance

As human systems are implemented and operated, data are collected and compared with the standards, or evaluated. The result tells the manager how well employees in human services are performing. If they are performing to or above standard, there is little the manager needs to do other than reinforce the responsible people and examine the performance standards to see if they were high enough. That is not to say the managers should not always try to achieve higher performance levels than specified; they should do so whenever that is feasible. If there is some question, evaluation techniques can be used to test feasibility. When performance is low or declining, the manager should become most concerned.

If performance standards are appropriate to the situation, the manager must find the right method or combination of methods for increasing performance. He may need to eliminate political pressures, constrain spending, allocate or develop additional resources, or replan certain procedures. Basically, however, the problem will be in motivating the staff to perform to the standards. Letting staff members determine performance standards, collect data, and evaluate performance will go a long way toward motivating them, especially when the information is shared with other staff.

Again, motivation is no recent development. In eighteenth-century Scotland, Robert Owen identified performance and correlated motivation of the worker with overall organizational efficiency. From the eighteenth century to the present time much has been written about motivation. Motivation has been and is a popular topic not only in business but in the human services as well. Most common is the complaint "Johnny is not motivated." We hear that in school and, that's right, right out there among the manager's staff. We even hear it about the managers.

Motivation as an issue is meaningless, however, unless someone asks the question "motivated to do what?" Suffice it to say at this point that the total sequence of functions in the general management model will need to be followed before a manager can really deal with motivation. The information he needs or will need to deal with it will be made available through the various functions. In some instances the administrator will not need to deal with motivation because of the needs and work habits of some staff. In other instances managers will have to deal with motivation because needs and work habits are not adequate and other needs intervene.

In short, operation and implementation of services are initiated by directive of the manager that says the services will begin on a certain date and at a certain time. Preparatory work in planning is used to determine what is to be done and what performance is considered to be standard. Performance information is collected and compared with the standards. Based on evaluation results, the manager makes certain changes and/or finds methods of motivating staff so that performance standards are met.

In essence, the general management tasks of the manager have been discussed in this subsection. What the manager does and how well he does it affects the overall performance of the organization. It would seem critical, then, that each manager pull together the technical base needed to manage that for which he is responsible and integrate it into his own unique management model.

Effect of the Interdisciplinary Approach

A predominant trend in today's professions is specialization. Professions or disciplines are subdivided. In medicine, for example, the general practitioner has become less and less abundant and such specialists as internists, orthopedic surgeons, and gynecologists have become more abundant. For the most part this specialization is due to technical developments that enable an individual to become highly competent within a limited area. An individual who has specialized can perform services that a generalist is seldom capable of providing.

Specialization has led to a high degree of productivity and has been a major contributing factor to the United States' technical development and standard of living. However, a major problem is due to specialization: lack of overall control and coordination. Professional specialization, in many cases, has created a need for managers to coordinate the work of specialists. Simon describes professional specialization as being on a horizontal plane, whereas management of the specialties is on a vertical plane. A means of maintaining the horizontal plane is needed, and that is a job for management.

A narrow approach can be created in a specialty area or even within a single profession. In human services, there are those who believe that a profession (social work, psychology, or medicine) or a specialty area (diagnosis and evaluation, behavioral modification, vocational counseling) is the answer to the total problem. Administrators who have been promoted to management positions after training and/or heavy involvement in professions or specialty areas sometimes take such a narrow view that their management capability on the horizontal plane is severely restricted. Two approaches are currently being used to unite numerous professions or specialty areas and focus attention on a specific problem, objective, or consumer. These are the interdisciplinary and transdisciplinary approach and the systems approach.

The interdisciplinary and transdisciplinary approach is used to focus the attention of a number of professionals or specialists on a client or patient or a particular problem within the system. Once primary diagnosis and evaluation are completed, various professionals or specialists address the areas of requisite remediation detected through diagnosis and evaluation. After an initial screening, they conduct a more detailed diagnosis and evaluation, and the information is compiled and presented to an interdisciplinary team. At this point, recommendations from the various specialists are compiled in a consumer or system program plan and are used to meet a particular need. The content of the plan is then implemented. Plans and progress are then reviewed in interdisciplinary meetings and further changes are enacted as needed.

The key element in the interdisciplinary and transdisciplinary process is the program plan. It provides a set of objectives aimed at improving the consumer's lifestyle or the performance of the system. Improving lifestyle is the major objective of the organization from the consumer's standpoint, and the individual program plan becomes the staff's management tool for achieving the objective.

For the most part individual program plans have been used only for consumers; for managers at higher levels, however, they have unlimited uses. They can be used for staff program plans, departmental programs, and organizational program plans.

The systems approach, or one of the various corollaries of that approach, is also used to allow various professionals or specialists to concentrate on a common problem. Steps within the approach include:

Problem definition or needs assessment.
Alternative solution development.
Solution selection.
Solution tryout.
Solution implementation.
Evaluation and feedback.

The approach requires not only the use of varied professions and resources but also an optimal balance or combination in what is considered to be the most effective and efficient manner.

The systems approach differs somewhat from the interdisciplinary and transdisciplinary approach in that it calls for a number of alternatives and a high degree of solution development, selection, and performance evaluation. It has been more readily used in military and business sectors, where more effective tools have been developed for measuring performance. In human services, where performance has been more difficult to measure, it has been less effective. However, the systems approach can and should be applied to human services. Further discussion of its application is included in Chapter 2.

The Impact of Social Philosophies

The impact of social philosophies on human services is of key importance. Products of human services have been found to be directly linked to timely philosophies. Philosophy provides the guiding force in an organization's or system's development. It provides direction for the establishment of goals as well as for resulting operational procedures. For example, in Nazi Germany, philosophies concerning a master race created "inhumane human services" such as the Germanization of children from occupied countries: children were separated from parents in occupied countries, classified according to German characteristics, placed in Germanization camps, and later placed with German citizens who did not have children. No single nation is without such examples. In the United States, institutional philosophies have created dehumanizing conditions that are bringing about major lawsuits. Such publications as *Christmas in Purgatory* depict the subjection of American citizens to institutional conditions little different from those in concentration camps.

In countries sincere about improving human services, traditional benevolent-autocratic philosophies appear to be declining. That is evidenced in social philosophies concerned with the effect of services on the consumer. The recent trends in accountability, normalization, and human rights in this country reflect definite concern for individual consumers and for human service performance. Although the federal government has not always specified how the concepts might best be applied, procedures appear to include the use of quantitative data for evaluation and improvement of human services. It would be good if the trend became reality and was not reduced to a mere catch word or fad.

It is critical to note that the management of program and cost performance is a *process*. It can be used to manage human services effectively and efficiently. It can also be used to manage services that are humane and that truly meet the needs of a target population. Elemental in this is the concept that no human service system is complete without its philosophy and ideology, nor is it complete unless it manages performance effectively. Those are essential components.

Conclusion

There is an abundance of reasons why human service managers should be effective. There is also some good evidence, including consumer dissatisfaction and tax-payer dissatisfaction, that our human services are not getting the job done. Two reasons are poor direction and poor performance within human services. Effective management of human services is not the whole answer, but it is a major one. It is also the key to success for the individual, and it can have an effect on the overall good of the country. In coming years, there will be even a greater need for effective managers.

The key to effective management is the individual management model that the manager develops to fit his unique situation. Management models are unique not only to the type of service but to the changing environment in and around the human service system. In this respect, they must be dynamic and ever-changing.

In order for a manager to develop a unique model, it is

necessary for him to draw from a wide range of concepts, principles, strategies, tools, and procedures that will provide solutions for individual management need. The concepts, and so on, will then need to be integrated into a comprehensive structure. Technology for both tools and procedures are contained in the text.

Improvement in the direction and performance of human services is a necessity. Change and improvement in services must be well planned and controlled over a period of time. Just as it is not possible to build a skyscraper or develop a career in one day, so it is not possible to implement changes overnight. Even with the best planning and control, however, implementation of change and improvement can be problematic. But the administrator can diminish the problems inherent in implementing changes by improving his philosophical references and the tools and techniques that he employs.

2

A foundation for formative management

If the administrator of a human service system is to be a leader and manager of that system rather than a hole patcher or defensive bureaucrat, he will need to turn the tide within his organization. As in sports, he must be able to perceive himself as the offensive coordinator of the team rather than as the defensive safety. His philosophy, role, and skills will need modification, and he must start by building a philosophical foundation from which he can develop new concepts and skills. The following pages describe a number of principles and techniques which have utility in building a management foundation and introduce a particular form of management: formative management.

Guiding Management Principles

Numerous management principles have been formulated to date. Managers often formulate principles that are unique to certain situations, and those principles are sometimes concerned with political gain, personal gain, empire building, survival, or isolationism. All too infrequently are they concerned with human need, performance, productivity, and human rights. Principles serve as a foundation for the manager, and they are the basis for methods applied in managing a human service system. The following list of principles is incomplete, but it does provide a core for use in improving the direction and performance of human service organizations.

Offensive management

Throughout this country's history, various groups, organizations, and businesses have made their largest gains by using offensive tactics. Yet a group's offensive thrusts must be designed to produce maximum gains at minimum cost. Priorities must be assessed, goals determined, and strategies implemented. Continual planning and evaluation are essential to a successful offensive campaign. Managers must think of themselves as on the offensive in providing services for such clients as children, handicapped persons, the destitute, elderly, and ill; for those clients are not able to fight battles for themselves. The responsibility for providing services is primarily that of the administrator; for, as a commanding officer, he is responsible to all those whom he serves. The principle of offensive management, then, involves the continual and systematic exertion of effective tactics and methods to improve the human service system.

Consumer need

In recent years, allegations have been made to the effect that human service systems are nothing more than "middle class welfare systems": they meet the needs of the middle class rather than those of the intended consumer by paying high salaries within the system. The allegations have some substance when human service managers are paid high salaries and provide inferior, dehumanizing services. A parallel exists in the business world; when management salaries become top-heavy but performance and profits decrease, personnel must be reduced. A common solution to the problem in business is the elimination of middle management in an attempt to streamline the business and improve efficiency. Today there is a premium on top managers who are able to improve an organization's overall productivity. The improved performance encompasses not only an increased quantity but also an increased quality of goods produced to meet the consumers' demand.

Accordingly, determining consumer need is a critical requisite for developing service systems that are responsive. Insight on the part of management is necessary to determine and define consumer needs. For instance, a human service system might stop defining needs by the number of supportive services and processes such as counseling, social work, and transportation and begin defining needs by change in life environments (independent living environments, supportive work environments, institutional prevention environments). Traditional supportive services might or might not be required. Again there is a parallel in the business world. If a business were to ignore the principle, consumers might, say, still be driving Model-T Fords—provided the business were able to survive at all without meeting updated consumer demands.

Quantitative measurement

It is not unusual to hear the generalization, "Human beings are too complex in their needs and desires, and service to them just cannot be measured." But although that might be heard from a social worker, it would doubtfully be heard from a tailor, who also provides services to consumers. The tailor must be able to produce clothing that meets the consumer's needs as to type, quality, and economy. He can certainly measure his performance by the types of clothing purchased, the quantity and kinds of goods used, and the cost of items most frequently purchased. Why, then, is it not possible for the social worker to determine types of services and products that must be provided, necessary quality of services, and reasonable costs for the services? The answer is that such measurements are not typically required in nonbusiness human services. Organizations are funded only for the provision of services; cost is based on an overall budget; and performance is typically not an issue. This answer is also due to the fact that measurement techniques and tools either have not been developed or have not been fully implemented in human services.

There are two problems in the area of quantification of human services: product criteria and product frequency. Criteria for the dimensions of service products must be fairly precise so that service products will be measured consistently with the desired degree of accuracy, and they must be sufficiently clear that it is possible to determine whether actual service products meet them. A service unit may truly be counted as a "product" only when it has met criteria.

Second, the frequency with which service products are provided must be clearly quantified. Only when service products are measured systematically can the quantitative approach to evaluation and decision making be used.

Product, process, and cost

The primary mission of human service system has been to provide services that meet the needs of the individuals to whom the services are responsible. A service system must be viewed in practical terms as a process that is similar in many respects to, say, the manufacture of automobiles. The product of the human service system is the change in the individual's lifestyle, or a change in the deficit which restricts a normal lifestyle. In business, cost can be attached to both product and process in order to measure effectiveness of services in dollars. Similarly, in human services the product-process-cost principle requires that an organization must define the products of human services, determine the best means of production, and produce the products efficiently. Figure 2-1 is an example of an input-output model that illustrates the principle of product, process, and cost.

Major indicators

At all levels of service organizations, it is necessary to specify products, processes, and cost criteria if information for quantitative evaluation is to be obtained. At various levels and in various components of the human ser-

Figure 2-I.   Input-output model.

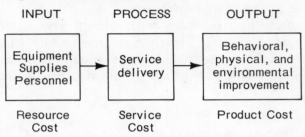

vice system, product, process, and cost information can be a tremendous asset. However, it simply is neither feasible nor efficient to combine all data into one set of information. To follow our metaphor, the president of General Motors does not need to know if every hole drilled in the fender of an automobile meets criteria, although the foreman of the department must know. The president needs other kinds of information as the basis for decisions, such as number of automobiles produced according to a certain standard.

The problem is found in human services as well. Stufflebeam states:

> It must be realized that today the field of evaluation is complex, and describing every decision sequence in a system will only lead to confusion.

He goes on to say:

> Obviously, all of the possible data that could be and are generated (for conceptual purposes) at the lowest level of

our educational system could not be transmitted to national decision makers.

What managers must do is to determine the functional pieces of information that they need at their level. They must determine the major indicators that tell them what they need to know about the organization's overall performance. Major indicators function much like the warning lights in an automobile that tell the driver when there are major problems. Other evaluation instruments are then used to determine the specific problem. The best use of major indicators, however, is to determine how good the performance is.

Humanization and normalization

Management must include a humanization and a normalization philosophy. That is as important for the consumer of human services as it is for the providers and managers of the services. Consumers should be afforded the rights of all citizens. But when, in a mental retardation institution, a superintendent's dog bit a patient, the patient rather than the dog was confined for observation. The girl, and not the dog, was punished for the incident! The ease with which management and staff may dehumanize consumers of human services must not confuse the issue: Clearly, human services are provided for the consumer, not for the convenience of the human service organization.

However, staff and management in human service organizations also can be subjected to dehumanization. Managers who read staff mail, who do not consider staff ideas, and who use their authority to attack or condemn without reason practice dehumanization in an obvious form. Similarly, there are staff who unfairly blame administrators for their own inadequacies.

The wise manager accepts the humanity of consumers and staff and treats each accordingly. Similarly, staff must view their managers as human beings. When those attitudes do not prevail, inhumane treatment leads to anger, apathy, resentment, insecurity, fear, and often low performance. The principle of humanization and normalization is of key importance to the human service organization—to all organizations.

Concentrated power

The individuals who control an organization may or may not be found on the table of organization. Sometimes the actual leaders are strong subordinates with independent goals who influence their co-workers. Administrators can be ineffective because they are unable to control subordinate staff. The difficulty rests on the administrator's inability to see that power is not always exercised by those who are granted authority. The power of a manager who is not a leader is most often usurped by an unofficial leader who gains organizational control. Effective managers are actual leaders who develop the power to manage their immediate staff who in turn manage others.

Thus the key to effective management is not autocratic control; instead, it is leadership. In essence, the principle of concentrated power is the management (planning, coordination, organization, and control) of organizational leaders in order to improve the direction and performance of the entire organization. In this way, the power and expertise of a few is channeled to lead the many.

Congruent need

It is not uncommon for an administrator to explain poor performance by lack of motivation. Motivation has been the subject of numerous books, and a considerable quantity of research on it has been conducted. Popular theories of motivation are concerned with behavioral science and specifically with the needs of individual workers. Primary and secondary needs and need hierarchies were first delineated by Maslow, whose pioneering work has been expanded to explain organizational behavior. Herzberg noted that individuals have a variety of needs; he developed his "motivational hygiene theory" to explain and predict the policies and practices that can be used to acquire, maintain, and motivate desirable employees.

The Getzels-Guba model is used to explain how individual personality and need disposition impel an individual to exhibit behavior that may not be consistent with that of the organization. An individual, then, may be motivated to fulfill his own needs, but the needs fulfillment process and his resulting behavior may not be congruent with the behaviors of the organization.

If individual needs do not coincide with needs of the organization, the individual must be placed in a situation such that his own needs and those of the organization are congruent. However, organizational needs must prevail over individual needs, and if the difference between the two is too great, the staff member may have to be terminated.

Formative management

Reference is often made to the formative years of life, when skills and personality are developed. Similarly, a human service system has formative years. As with the individual, they are the early years, yet the formative process continues during the system's span of life. Thus the principle of formative management emphasizes the shaping and molding of organizational behavior to meet the needs of the individuals to whom the organization is responsible. The formative process within human service systems parallels that of the child. The ultimate outcome is due primarily to the environment that is provided. The environment can be planned, implemented, and constantly improved to meet the needs of the child. The process can be used for the human service organization as well.

Dimensions of Organizational Performance

"Behavior" commonly refers to one's conduct. The command "You behave!" means, in parental terms, that a child should not do something that has been forbidden him. Thus a child's behavior may be considered "good" or "bad" according to his response to parental standards.

Also, behavior is typically confined to observable events: society punishes individuals for actual crimes rather than for intent to commit crimes. Accordingly, society considers frequent occurrence of certain behaviors more serious than behaviors that occur only once. Conversely, individuals are acknowledged by society for committing "good" acts. Again, intentions to commit good acts are never acknowledged by society, although society does recognize incremental good acts. Organizations are composed of human beings who have collective standards and exhibit collective behavior. Accordingly, collective "good" and "bad" behaviors are found in organizations.

Organizational Products

Various individuals within an organization emit similar behavior which, when quantified, constitutes organizational behavior. For example, if an employment office processed 200 applications, an application processed by an individual could be considered as an organizational behavior. The 200 applications that were processed by 25 employees could be considered total organizational behavior for the day. A single organizational behavior, when defined with a criterion, can be designated as an organizational product, referred to here as a "service product" (one processed application). Products in a defined period of time are referred to as organizational behavior (200 processed applications).

In effect, a manager and staff must analyze the organization and designate service products. They must then quantify the products for a predetermined period and compare them with a standard in order to evaluate organizational behavior. For example, when the nurse of a preschool provides a general examination of 22 preschoolers each day, one examination could be defined as a service product. If the time period to be used were a single day, the number of general examinations each day would constitute organizational behavior. Quantity will vary over time. Figure 2-2 is an example of how to chart quantitative measurements over time.

Figure 2-2. Quantity organizational behavior charted over a week.

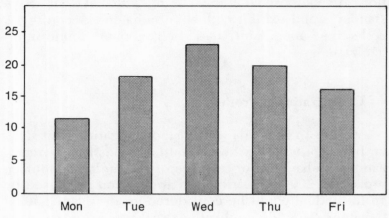

Differentiation of Quality and Quantity

Organizational behavior has been described as the quantification of service products. However, quantity is but one dimension of total behavior. Quality is the second dimension, and both quality and quantity should be used to evaluate organizational behavior effectively. For example, if the eyes, ears, and throat of each preschooler in the preceding example were to be examined and if any of those areas were not examined, the examination would be considered of inferior quality. In a human service organization, it could be considered a "reject," and not be counted. When both quantity and quality, as of examinations, are considered, organizational behavior can be analyzed for any single day or over the period of a week. As with quantity, quality will vary over time. Fig-

Figure 2-3. Quality and quantity behavior charted over a week.

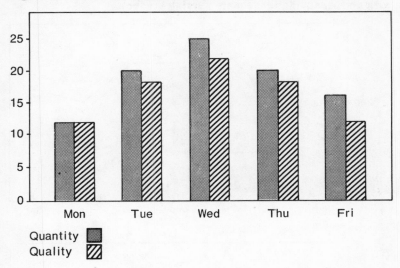

Quantity ▒
Quality ▨

ure 2-3 is an example of how to chart quality and quantity data over time.

In the preceding example the quality dimension of
the examination was differentiated by using a subquantity of three (eyes, ears, and throat). It would be possible
to break the three components down into subcomponents in order to measure quality even more accurately.

It is often said that quality is a subjective judgment
made by each individual. Philosophically, it might be
argued that any time a number is attached to some aspect
of the product, quality no longer exists. Programmati-
cally speaking, if a subquantity is not attached to a product, quality cannot be measured with any degree of precision. With that in mind, it should be concluded, at least
for the purpose of this chapter, that quality is defined by
identifying the type and number of components within a

Figure 2-4. Quantity and quality of nursing products charted with corresponding inadequate nursing products.

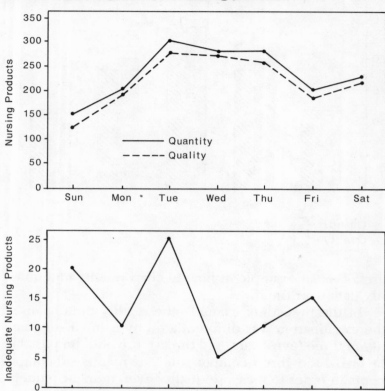

service product and the type and number of subcomponents within components if needed. The organization must decide the level of subquantities used to define quality in a way that is most beneficial to it. However, quality cannot be defined with numbers alone; verbal descriptions are needed to supplement numeric descriptions. This concept is discussed in further detail in the section on measurable objectives.

Figure 2-4 is an example of organizational behavior. A nurse supervisor charted the number of staff nursing skills performed (service product quantity), the number of skills performed to criteria (service product quality), and the number of skills performed that did not meet criteria (service product rejects). During the seven-day period over which the data were charted, the pattern of organizational behavior can be analyzed.

Organizational Behavior Versus Performance

If one observed a halfback playing in the Super Bowl, at least one aspect of behavior could be measured by yards of rushing. The back's performance, however, could be measured only if it were compared with some standard such as the 100-yard performance standard. More yards than that would be considered greater performance, and fewer yards would be considered inferior performance. Similarly, when behavior is compared with a standard, the results of the comparison yield performance information. Lower quantities and qualities indicate low performance; equal quantities and qualities indicate average or standard performance; and higher quantities and qualities indicate high performance. Performance, then, is determined by a comparison of organizational behavior with a performance standard. Both the quality and quantity of organizational behavior can be measured if quality and quantity performance standards are established.

In our earlier example, the organizational behavior (200 processed unemployment applications) may be

Figure 2-5. Quality, quantity, and cost performance evaluation.

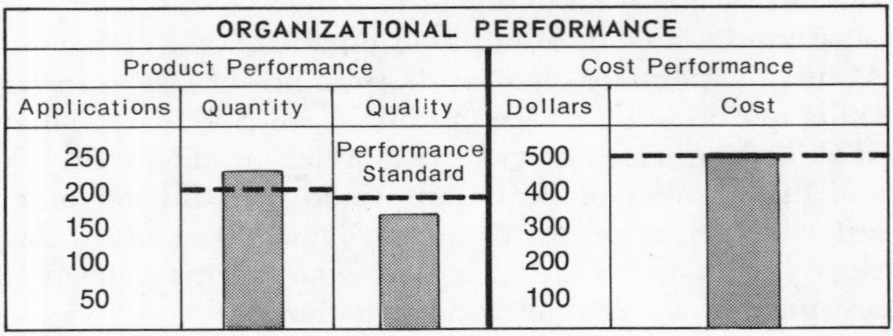

ORGANIZATIONAL PERFORMANCE				
Product Performance			Cost Performance	
Applications	Quantity	Quality	Dollars	Cost
250		Performance Standard	500	
200			400	
150			300	
100			200	
50			100	

considered good or poor performance depending upon whether the daily performance standard is 150 or 300. If 70 percent of the required items on a single application were filled out correctly, quality could be rated poor or good depending on whether the standard was 90 percent or 50 percent. If the standard were set at 90 percent, all of the applications that were filled out with less than 90 percent accuracy could be rejected because of low quality. In Figure 2-5, the quantity performance standard for processing applications was set at 200 and the quality standard was set at 190; a difference of 5 percent was set as the rejection level.

Cost Performance

In addition to product performance, which involves the comparison of service product qualities and quantities with performance standards, there is cost performance. Cost performance is derived by simply comparing cost of products with a cost standard. In this instance, the dollar serves as the measure. Correspondingly, the number of dollars spent serves as the organizational behavior, and the comparison of dollars spent with the standard number of dollars allotted determines performance. If the cost standard is $500 and the actual cost, or the organizational behavior, also is $500, cost performance is neither high nor low, but standard.

In summary, in order to define organizational performance, it is necessary to define organizational behavior (quantity, quality, and cost of service products). The first major delineation of performance is that of product cost. Product performance can be further separated into quantity and quality. As Figure 2-5 shows, quantity, quality, and cost can be compared to related standards and evaluated on one chart to determine low, standard, or high performance. In effect, organizational behavior is organizational performance if it is evaluated in the light of a certain organizational performance standard. Generally, it is management's task to insure that organizational behavior is controlled, molded, and shaped to conform to or exceed the standard.

Formative Management

If one were to observe a child's behavior and objectify his view, it would not be necessary to describe the child with some stereotype such as incorrigible beast, goody two-shoes, or hoodlum. The child's development, with corresponding formative social, academic, and religious development, must be considered as unacceptable and acceptable behavior. Behavior that is unacceptable by some standard is to be decreased, and behavior that is considered acceptable is to be maintained or increased. The child is primarily a product of his environment, and those who are responsible for his development must view their mission as one of molding and shaping his behavior. The process is a continuous one in which both long-range goals and immediate objectives are set for the child. Depending upon the child and the situation, the goals, objectives, and the shaping process are adjusted.

For example, a family might set the goal of a high school education with an emphasis on business for their daughter. Their immediate objective might be for her to complete the eighth grade, in which she was enrolled in a general preparatory program. Perhaps during that year, she might skip her math class but also make outstanding grades in her art class. Now, if the managers (that is, parents, teacher, principal, and counselor) viewed the girl as a disobedient child and sought only to punish her, they would be reacting only to the critical incidents that had occurred (such as skipping math class). They should be concerned with the overall shaping and molding process: setting new possible goals (perhaps a college education in fine arts) and setting up an academic program that parallels an art career.

This is not to say that skipping math class should be condoned. We must live with the consequences of our actions. Our hypothetical girl must suffer the consequences of skipping math classes, but, more important, there must be an effort to capitalize on individual talents and to mold and shape those talents. A critical incident such as skipping a class is much less important than the overall behavior that is to be molded and shaped.

The view of behavior in the preceding example is one that is basically objective and comprehensive. Children exhibit behavior that can be compared with standards. Similarly, human service organizations exhibit behavior. When an organization sets its goals and develops measurable objectives based on those goals, organizational behavior can be compared with performance criteria or performance standards. When it differs from the standard, it can be considered as higher or lower performance. When the performance of the organization differs greatly from the standard, it can be considered to be extremely high or low.

In actuality, organizational behavior is simply a product of its environment. Managers should be able to modify the environment of a human service organization in order to mold and shape organizational behavior so that the objectives and goals of the organization are met. Sometimes it is necessary to overlook slightly undesirable behavior for a time in order to achieve high performance. Furthermore, managers must insure that their goals and objectives are based upon consumer need. The process of modifying the environment and molding and shaping organizational behavior in a manner that meets consumer need should be considered as a formulative process or "formative management."

To elaborate, if the objective of a social service agency were to reduce the number of elderly persons living in nursing homes while maintaining a high level of care, the resulting product would be considered the person living in a nursing home. If the number of occupants in a nursing home per month were tabulated, one might find that there was an average of 20. If in March the management set the standard as 15 per month and instituted meals-on-wheels and visiting-nurses programs for senior citizens, the frequency of products might well begin to decline toward the standard.

The organizational behavior in this case could be molded and shaped to a level that was more acceptable. Living in a nursing home certainly is not what might be considered normal, and reducing the incidence of premature confinement where possible by increasing organizational behavior (service delivery) would certainly be in the best interest of the consumer population.

Cost behavior would be affected by the changes in service delivery. If the cost of the meals-on-wheels and visiting-nurses programs were less than per diem costs of the confined elderly persons, the overall costs would certainly decrease. They might not decrease as rapidly as could be wished when the meals-on-wheels and visiting-nurses programs were first implemented, because of implementation costs, but they could be reduced in time. In this example the objective would be to mold and shape the overall behavior of the organization to reduce both the number of nursing home residents and the cost of their care while bettering the quality of life.

Financial Contingencies and Formative Management

The means by which a human service organization obtains its funding inevitably places restrictions upon it. If funds are paid to the organization for providing psychiatric service, a psychiatric staff and the presence of clients in the facility are basically all that is necessary to receive funding. The contingency, then, is that if one sets up and provides services, one receives a yearly budget. In this situation, the contingency does not go beyond the process of establishing and providing services. However, in formative management, establishing and providing services is not sufficient. Major products that will improve the health, education, or welfare of the client must be defined. Although the funding source requires only that services be provided, formative management requires that service products be defined quantitatively and qualitatively, compared, and modified as necessary to meet the consumer's need.

The management of an organization would certainly act differently if the organization were funded on the basis of the quality and quantity of service products. If in a school the number of disadvantaged students being educated were viewed as the product and the teachers and administrators were paid accordingly, both the faculty view of the student and the educational methods used might be modified radically. Contrary to current situations, both teachers and administrators might concentrate on how to educate the students effectively rather than on how to make them drop out. In this instance, the administrators and teachers would then probably stop complaining about how difficult it is to measure quality and quantity of products and would simply begin the measurements in order to receive funds. They might become more concerned about integration and an effective and efficient educational program than about the poor behavior and performance of students.

(It must be noted that the above example is not a criticism of administrators or teachers in general. The author spent a number of years teaching in a disadvantaged school and recognizes the restraints imposed by funding contingencies. Rather, criticism here is directed at the contingency link of funding for the services process and the inequities that it produces.)

In some human service organizations, however, the contingency link in human services is money and products. When a nursing home is paid on the basis of the number of patients in it, per diem rates for the number of patients serve as the contingency link. If both administrators and staff are paid on that basis, it is undoubtedly in the best financial interests of the organization to maintain a high number of patients. Here the product is defined as patients occupying space, and it is inferior because it does not answer the question, "Does the product truly improve the consumer's lifestyle?" Some human service organizations might maintain patients or even impede treatment in order to keep a sizable number of patients and thereby maintain full production and reduce operating costs.

The product in this example would need to be redefined in such a way that there could be some improvement in the clients' lifestyles instead of mere "warehousing." Products might be defined as both occupancy and improvement, or, in some cases, a reduction in the rate of developmental or physical deterioration. In the nursing home example, the service agency managers instituted meals-on-wheels and visiting-nurses programs, and they thereby improved the lifestyle of their elderly citizens while reducing costs. There definitely must be a contingency link that rewards improvement in lifestyle and performance. Contingency links that improve performance in a similar manner are integral to the concept of formative management.

Formative Management and Organizational Complexities

The growing complexities of human service organizations present an enormous problem. We typically describe such organizations as systems—an educational system, a welfare system, and a health care system. Human service managers traditionally establish tables of organization that define the systems as authoritative hierarchies, not services. Tables of organization and, usually, lists of facilities and job descriptions are the major tools used in defining service systems. Such tools have a place, but they must be supplemented by other, functional management tools. Sometimes the consumers (citizens of the state, students of the community, patients of the hospitals) are listed at the tops of the tables of organization, but their rights and needs and their input are typically considered to a far lesser degree. Figure 2-6 represents a general table of organization. Political decision makers are at the higher level of authority, followed by government administrators and then service managers and providers. Far below that structure the consumer assumes his poorly defined place.

The table of organization is typically used to reduce complexities by defining organizational levels and the authoritative relations between levels and their span of control. It does not address such other critical questions as what the organization's service products are. Nor does it address the problem of coordinating, evaluating, and managing the process or cost. Tables of organizations can be used to illustrate hierarchical authority, but that is not enough. Managers must be responsible to consumer populations for delivery of products and for economy and improvement of the system. Tables of organization cannot be used effectively to illustrate the flow of services or service products to consumers, yet they are the principal planning diagrams used by most human service managers today. Some of the more effective techniques that must be used to define the human service system are described in Chapter 3.

Figure 2-6. General human services table of organization.

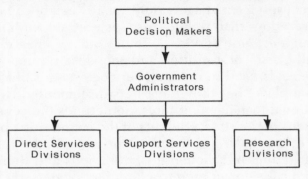

If a manager is to mold and shape organizational behavior, he must be able to define the products of the
service system. He must have the technical capability to
develop human service "blueprints" that will reduce organizational complexity. He must be able to define and
communicate the total system accurately. First, the
boundary of the human service organization is established, and then various service products and components of the organizational system are defined. Next, the
flow to and through the components as well as the inter-
relations of the components are defined. Resources and
personnel are then assigned to the components, and
managers are made responsible for performance within
the components (that is, responsibility centers are established). Overall management (that is, the total responsibility center and the overall products and costs) is the
responsibility of top managers. By using the systems
blueprint it is possible to combine responsibility, authority, and product and process cost functions. Systems
blueprinting techniques can be used at all organizational
levels; by legislators, top managers, government de-

partment heads, agency heads, or ward supervisors.

Although a system blueprint or model can help define organizational authority, its basic utility lies in illustrating various human service components and how their service products are related. Direct service products are those produced by service components that provide direct services to consumers. Products used to support direct services are considered indirect products. Research and needs assessment products, as well as management products, are also indirect products.

For example, direct service could consist of a number of competency-based training programs used to improve the occupational skills of minority groups. Attainment of competence by each student in each instructional module could be used to define the *direct* service product. Other services—such as transporting students to a center or tabulating performance scores—constitute *indirect* service products. Such products as improved curricula, improved recruitment packages, and needs assessment reports for management can also be considered indirect products. Even within management, results of weekly planning, performance evaluations, grant applications, and think tanks can be considered indirect products. Accordingly, the dimensions of these products must be defined through objectives. Such product definition is further discussed in Chapter 4.

Formative Management and Humanization

An individual may find himself involved in a job such that, no matter how hard he works, he is frustrated. It has been the author's observation that this often occurs when an individual is not certain how well he is performing *or whether anyone cares about his performance.*

When there are no criteria for performance, an employee can become extremely frustrated. In fact, many employees are often more frustrated by lack of feedback concerning performance than they are by being overworked.

The following example illustrates how managers who are not concerned with performance frustrate employees as well as stifle performance. A young professional accepted the position of systems analyst in a human service organization. At about that time, a doctoral candidate who was completing his final year in a psychology program had been hired as a temporary manager. Following an interview, the manager instructed the new systems analyst to go to his new office but said nothing about his duties.

After an unreasonable period of idle waiting, the new employee returned to the manager's office in an agitated and frustrated state and demanded to know what his duties were to be. The manager was pleased by his employee's agitation; he said that the young man had now gained an anxiety level sufficient for productivity.

The employer's insensitivity demonstrated his lack of managerial and personal skills and his ignorance of productivity and performance. Apparently, he was more concerned with manipulating the young professional's anxiety level than with defining and evaluating performance. His management behavior was nonproductive, and his inhumanity illustrates a critical need for the development of managers who are both performance-minded and aware of the dignity of work and the needs of their employees as people.

Another concept that is inherent in formative management is that of participatory management. The employee who has no control over his destiny and who does not share in the responsibility for molding and shaping organizational behavior can often become frustrated. The employee should be allowed to plan with higher-level managers or carry out tasks that he believes will lead to higher productivity within the organization. If he thinks he can provide a better human service product or provide the product at less cost, he should have the opportunity and the responsibility to try. If he fails, he must accept responsibility for his actions.

On the other hand, although management must gamble somewhat on the outcome of the employee's performance, it must also minimize risk to the consumer. One way to minimize uncertainty and increase performance is to give an individual the opportunity to plan his performance contribution with higher-level managers and the authority to perform. If the manager is unwilling to provide for performance planning in a participatory manner, he has already begun to minimize performance and promote dehumanization.

Formative Management Effectiveness and Efficiency

In human service systems, the terms "effectiveness" and "efficiency" have often been used as if they were somewhat synonymous. Service providers are beginning to view effectiveness as the quantity and quality of service to the consumers and efficiency as the most equitable cost of providing the services. The two terms *are* related. However, effectiveness must be established before it is possible to determine efficiency.

For example, effectiveness could be defined as a service product such as a consumer in a mental retardation program being trained to eliminate in a toilet without assistance. The training program is, of course, the process, but effectiveness is based upon how often and how well the consumer performs. If the consumer is trained to perform with little or no assistance, the program can be considered effective. This same situation could apply for a parent who is toilet-training one of his or her own children. Parents must deal with the same kind of effectiveness.

Efficiency, on the other hand, is determined by the relation of cost to effect. Anthony states:

> Efficiency is used in an engineering sense—that is, the amount of output per unit of input. An efficient machine generates a given quantity of outputs with a minimum consumption of inputs or generates the longest possible output from a given quantity of inputs.

In human engineering or human services, Anthony's statement might be interpreted as meaning that a smaller amount of human service resource input produces the same number of human service products or that an existing amount of input produces a larger number of human service products.

The quantities of input can be directly related to cost, and smaller amounts of input or larger amounts of output therefore reduce the cost per product. In the example of a consumer being toilet-trained, several procedures could be used to produce the effect (toilet training). First, a ward attendant trying procedure A could be used. Second, a new treatment technique (procedure B) could be used. And finally, an automatic toilet-training machine (procedure C) could be used. If all three procedures produced the same effect (toilet training to criteria), one of them would probably be less costly. In other words, one of the procedures would probably be more efficient than the other two.

Managers should be careful to collect a complete set of data in order to determine efficiency. Figure 2-7 is a hypothetical example of a method of comparing efficiency data. The automated procedure, C, required fewer hours of training time. However, the average training cost is only part of the picture. When procedure C is used, the cost of the expensive automated resources and their maintenance must be included. When the actual costs of the three procedures are compared, B appears to be most efficient.

The overall task of the manager is to create an optimum balance of product effectiveness and efficiency, preferably weighted in that order. Contrarily, a traditional expectation of a human service system is to be all things to all people! When a human service system falls short of that goal, it becomes open to criticism. In actuality, such a goal as "the highest level of normal living," "the ultimate development of the child," or "comprehensive services" serves well. However, it must be reduced to measurable objectives and products that can be provided realistically and, more importantly, to which costs can be attached. The manager's job is to

Figure 2-7. Efficiency comparison of three training procedures.

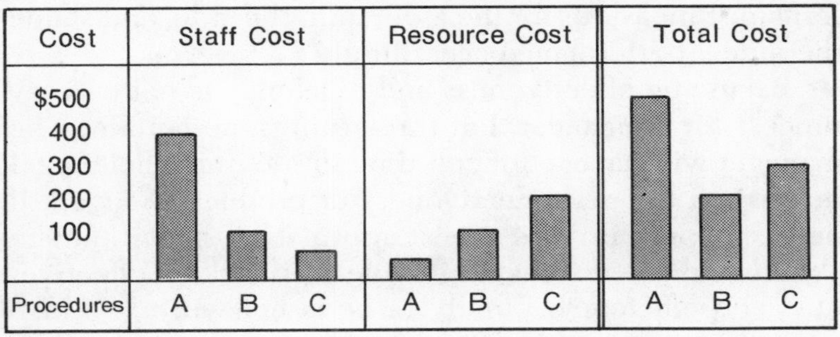

Cost	Staff Cost			Resource Cost			Total Cost		
$500 400 300 200 100									
Procedures	A	B	C	A	B	C	A	B	C

change objectives, products, or effects as dictated by the level of funding and/or consumer need. Each time the situation is modified, whether for reasons of need or by increases or decreases in the budget, it is the manager's job to balance effectiveness and efficiency at an acceptable level. The human service manager who tries to do all things for all people will soon fall short of such an overall goal.

Sometimes it is not easy to balance effectiveness and efficiency. For example, if a psychologist were to describe effect as a 100 percent accurately scored individual test, he might try several procedures to reduce the cost. He might score the tests himself, use an aide, or use a machine. If scoring by the machine or by the psychologist were 100 percent accurate and scoring by the aide were 80 percent accurate, and if the cost of scoring by the machine or by the psychologist were 50 percent higher, a decision concerning effectiveness and efficiency would need to be made. It would seem that there are two alternatives: (1) maintain the high rate of accuracy and high rate of cost or (2) reduce the requirement for a high rate of accuracy and maintain an acceptable cost level. As an old saying goes, however, "There are always more than two alternatives." What the psychologist might choose to do would be to set up performance measures for the aide, train the aide, and shape the aide's performance accordingly.

Balancing effectiveness and efficiency is not an easy process for a manager, but three things are certain: The manager will have a difficult time improving efficiency if he has not defined effectiveness or products. Second, if he has no performance or cost information, he will not be able to make decisions or provide feedback on effectiveness and efficiency. Finally, if he is not willing to take the time to define what he will do and how much he will spend, he has no recourse: All people might well expect all things from his system! He will find himself in the traditional predicament of having too little money and too much to do.

Formative Management: An Evolutionary Process

Throughout this text, certain concepts and procedures and their relations to formative management have been discussed. It must not be thought, however, that any of them are ultimate or unchangeable. Formative management is a process of molding and shaping the organization so that it meets the consumers' needs. As promising new management concepts and procedures are created, they should be tried within the human service system. If they are effective and efficient, they should be included. The educational or human service organization itself can often be the prime discoverer of improved concepts and procedures; for it is in the best position to both formulate and test innovations.

Human service managers must insure that the organization is innovative and future-oriented in this respect: They must reward not only those who are high performers but those who are innovative as well. Finally, they must be able to eliminate concepts and methods that are obsolete and/or create high costs, but they must make those judgments in light of consumer need and program and cost performance data yielded from the human service organization. The best improvements and innovations usually take place not through additions and sophistication, but through simplification.

Conclusion

If a manager is to mold and shape a human service system, he must have some foundation upon which he will build his management control system. In part, a good foundation can be developed with an understanding of formative management and management principles, a knowledge of the common dimensions of performance and cost, and an understanding of how both product and cost performance are applied in the real world. The foundation is also developed on the basis of an understanding of consumer needs, management technologies, and innovative thinking. Although some basic components of a management foundation are discussed here, they are by no means complete, and they should be expanded to fit the system for which the manager is responsible.

3

Defining and understanding human service systems

In past centuries, doctors bled the human body to rid it of disease; according to medical theory of the time, healing occurred only when excessive pressure in the body was reduced or eliminated. Obviously, physicians understood neither the functioning of the human body nor the effect of disease upon it. Consequently, if disease did not destroy the patient, the doctors' "cures" might.

Early architects were able to build only crude dwellings until it became possible to analyze the dimensions of a structure by reducing the total to smaller units whose relations to the whole building could be examined. Mass production too was made possible by analyzing the component parts of a particular product and studying how the parts could be put together. Many miracles of modern technology—production of the television, the splitting of the atom, fabrication of computers, landing a man on the moon, and construction of the World Trade Center—would not have been possible without the systematic reduction of complexities which allows things to be comprehended and controlled.

Thus the process of reducing complexities is one of dividing units into their component parts and finding the relations of the subunits to the whole units. Although that process has been used with a high degree of success in the "hard sciences," its application to human services has been markedly inadequate. If improvement in a human service system is desired, the component parts, or subunits, of the system must be delineated so that the total workings of the organization may be understood. Delineation of the component parts of a human service system is no more difficult than in a hard-science project. Simple lack of motivation and failure to use contingencies, rather than failure to understand technology, are the major impediments to explicit definition of human service systems.

The human service manager will find it extremely difficult to improve his system or solve its problems until he understands its intricate workings. Systems analysis, a method inherent in systems technology, is specifically designed to help the manager obtain a thorough understanding of his organization. Management application of the systems approach is described by Smith:

> In summary, *Systems Analysis* is the process of breaking things down. It is expressed as the requirement and factor needed to perform a mission. It provides management with the input of all that is involved in solving the problem. In essence, it is simulating the problem solution on paper, brainstorming, and studying to see if it is feasible before implementation. This approach creates communication tools and communication referents while helping to guide the organization in the steps of logical problem solving.

Definition and delineation of the system, then, is the initial step of the systems approach. Further, some form of modeling or blueprinting technique is required.

Utilization of systems models allows (1) definition of human service system boundaries, (2) identification of various system components, (3) identification of system component functions, and (4) identification of the relations between various components. Systems models are used in two major ways: to model the existing service system and to model the ideally improved system. In modeling an existing service system, that which exists within the system is identified and synthesized as a model. That kind of modeling leads logically to the second kind of ideal modeling; the improved or ideal model is then used as the basis for improvements to the existing service system. Stufflebeam elaborates:

> A model in this sense is an ideal representation of the real world, the Platonic "essence" of what "should be." Analytic man monitors the real world and uses his model of *what should be* as the standard to which he can compare *what actually is,* so that when a discrepancy between his real world and his ideal world occurs, he knows it.

In human services, the process of defining components and designing models is largely a continuous one, and one that must involve personnel at various levels within the organization. In essence, a model becomes a plan that encompasses direction and criteria for action. Subordinates involved in model development must also be involved in the model implementation process. Not only do they possess a real working knowledge of the model's respective components; they also will ultimately be given the responsibility to mold and shape the real world for which they are responsible so that it conforms to the ideal model.

Definition of the Human Service System

The initial steps required for defining the human service system involve securing a commitment, organizing resources, and preparing personnel. First, however, managers responsible for certain segments of the system or the overall system must determine that they will define the system and then commit their resources. Their communication that the system is to be defined is evidence that change in the daily routine of the organization is about to take place. Some subordinates will support change and even welcome it, but most will probably oppose it. Therefore, it is necessary that the managers' commitment be communicated and that managers persevere until the process is completed. If that does not occur, the system may well control the manager and any commitment to defining the system, much less molding and shaping it, will be lost.

Perseverance is not the only ingredient of implementation. Managers can advantageously use persuasive dialogues to sell the advantages of the desired improvements. They should make clear that the definition process is the first step. Implementation should not become a massive ordeal, and procedures should be absorbed by the system only at a rate at which they can be tolerated. Those who are most interested in adopting the initial procedures can often be used as a model for others to follow. Even those who resist the change should not be viewed as being irreconcilable. When procedures are implemented and the resisting staff see their utility and become proficient at using them, the resistors will often become some of the best proponents. In such an instance, a combination of education and persuasion is appropriate.

Resources needed to define the system depend, of course, upon the size of the system, but certain resources are essential. The first need is for personnel who possess the skills needed to define the system. It is possible to use a consultant, hire a staff person, and/or train existing managers presently on the staff. It is often best, initially, to use a third party as a resource to work with the group when analyzing the system. Eventually, managers and staff should be able to carry out the process independently. Procedures should become a routine component of the management system.

Finally, someone must be made responsible for the planning and utilization process. It will be necessary for that person to keep the process moving, help certain personnel with problems, and serve as the workforce for completing the final planning product. The responsibility will rest with top management, but in larger systems the authority is typically delegated to personnel who are accepted, competent, and committed and who have the authority and time to make arrangements and integrate the paperwork.

Defining a Human Service System

Two general approaches are used to define the service system; they are the analytic and the synthetic approaches. When the system is defined with the analytic approach, the overall system is defined and, through the analysis, reduced to detailed components. When the system is defined with the synthetic approach, detailed components of the system are defined and synthesized into the overall system. Both approaches are typically used throughout the definition process, often concurrently.

Boundaries

The first step in defining the human service system is to determine the boundaries of the system. That process requires the identification of physical facilities, physical resources, personnel, funding sources, finances, responsibility and authority areas, consumer groups, affiliated organizations, and other components that are within the jurisdiction and scope of human service system control. Often the boundaries of the real system are not the same as those that are designated or authorized in the organization's formal structure. Also, it is not always possible to identify completely all components within the boundaries. As the definition process is implemented, missing components can be added. Finally, it must be remembered that the boundaries of a service system are never constant. New finances, changes in administration and consumer populations, and modified policies are factors that can change the boundaries of the service system.

Mission

Defining the organization's mission may seem to be a simple and unimportant task, but it can have far-reaching effects. The mission statement can be used as the guidance core for the service system and dictate the direction in which the system should go. The importance of the mission statement is not its uniqueness but whether it is used to mold and shape the organization. Some human service organizations have beautifully written mission statements or goals; but when the system is analyzed, it is difficult to see any relation between operation and mission.

In drafting the mission statement, it is first necessary to define the consumer group served. At this point, a statement outlining needs to be met is formulated, and it is combined with the description of the consumer group. An example of a mission statement might be "to bring about a human service system that provides, through the creation and application of technology and human resources, a normal lifestyle for all persons who are developmentally disabled." Mission statements do not need to be wordy: A well-known cosmetic company's mission statement is simply "Hope for women." Mission statements should be formulated and accepted by all members of the system; everyone should have an opportunity to participate and to voice his ideas.

In certain instances, mission statements alone are insufficient, and "mission profiles" must be used. Smith elaborates:

> This technique calls for an expansion of the mission statement in terms of what the system is to accomplish. This includes descriptions of functions to be performed and to meet a specific need. Mission profiles can include sequences and time tables for the functions.

Defining the mission, then, is the second step. Over time, as the system requires change, the mission statement will have to be changed. New ideas, mandates, technological advancements, and new consumer populations may require certain modifications in the statement.

If the statement cannot be finalized initially, it should not be abandoned; instead it should be formulated throughout the definition process.

Goals and objectives

There is much literature on the subject of writing goals and objectives. In recent years, the use of measurable objectives within human services has received wide acceptance. Measurable objectives have been structured into competency-based training systems, for example. These innovations are highly desirable at both the operational and the top-management level. However, a difficulty is that measurable objectives are infrequently used at the top-management level in human service systems. Managers are often more concerned with goals and politics and do not break the goals down into measurable objectives.

Organizational goals constitute the first breakdown of the mission statement and can be based upon a mission profile. Typically, goals do not include precise measures but instead are general statements concerning overall functions to be performed. Once goals are determined, they must be broken down into the numerous objectives used to accomplish them. If the organization is serious about measuring performance, criteria will have to be included within the objectives.

The basic difficulty in nonbusiness human services, however, is that measurable criteria typically are not included in planning phases and therefore cannot be used in subsequent operational and control phases. That lack of precision makes it difficult for managers to both define and evaluate the human service system in order to control performance.

Development of Criteria for Objectives

To determine criteria to be used within objectives, an understanding of the general process of developing criteria is needed. It is not uncommon to encounter some rationale against developing measurable criteria. Some elements of persuasion and education, and even a full cycle of planning, persuasion, education, development, and refinement, may be needed to implement the process of developing criteria. It should be anticipated that the human service organization that has not been involved in developing criteria will certainly struggle with this difficult task in the initial stages. Assistance in this instance is important, and it must be understood by everyone that it is *not* wrong to develop criteria that can be tested and refined. It *is* wrong, however, not to develop any criteria.

Like the organization, criteria will need to be changed periodically. Once they are specified to the best of a group's ability, they must be tested. It is not unusual for an organization to change them frequently initially; at a certain point, however, they will be so perfected that they can be used for a long period of time. Criteria must be compared with the real world. Results from their testing against reality should then be used for further refinement.

This is a process that must be continually used in the system, and criteria must always be subject to change as more accurate criteria are formulated, as the organization changes, as needs of consumers change, or as financing changes.

Objectives and criteria, then, must be used with some flexibility. Drucker elaborates:

But objectives that become a straightjacket do harm. Objectives are always based on expectations. And expectations are, at best, informed guesses. Objectives express an appraisal of factors that are largely outside the business and not under its control.

Drucker goes on to say that objectives should be used in a way similar to that in which airlines use schedules and flight plans: Flight plans are used to keep schedules; but as weather changes, plans and schedules are modified to provide safe transportation for passengers. Similarly, as needs change, objectives may need to be altered so that the best possible service is provided.

What to Include in Measurable Objectives

Measurable objectives are typically written to include three components:

1. The requirements or constraints.
2. The task or the action.
3. The measurable criteria.

Once a criterion is established, it can be considered a single product. Each time it is met, it can be counted or quantified. The typical human service measurable objective usually does not specify what a product is and does not separate the product dimensions of quality and quantity. Without those measures, it is impossible to develop performance standards. A measurable objective should include the givens, the objective task, quality criteria, product designation, quantity criteria, and an identifier for the objectives. More simply, one says,

"With this, do this, this well, with this product—and this many."

Figure 3-1 is an example of a measurable objective that might be written within a correctional system. This objective has an identification number (1.0), a given (12 selected model inmates), an objective task (establishing individual work release programs), quality criteria (matching of work skills, interest, and career level and firm orientation), the product designation (one placement), and quantity (four per month within three months). It should be noted that it is not possible or necessary or desirable to be totally precise when objectives are set at this top program design level. *Overall* product measures are provided, and other and more detailed criteria must be formulated down through lower organizational levels until the desired precision is reached. This is a process that lets planning be carried out down through lower organizational levels. Top managers must define the nature and limits of objectives for lower-level operations. In other words, policy making is carried out at the highest level, policy specialization

Figure 3-I. Strategic-level measurable objective for setting up a work release program.

MEASURABLE OBJECTIVE					
I.D.	With This	Do This	This Well	Product	This Many
1.0	12 selected model inmates.	Set up individual work release programs.	1. That match job skill level. 2. That match interest and career level. 3. Where placement form has undergone orientation.	1 placement	4 per month within the next three months.

at middle ranks, and work performance at lower ranks.

As suggested, the example in Figure 3-1 is what might be called a top-level objective. It contains certain quantifiable measures (12 inmates and 4 placements per month over a 3-month period) that top management considers reasonable and necessary. At this top level, however, it is uncertain what criteria could be used for model inmates, for matching job skill level with matching career and interest level, and for providing placement firm orientation. In this situation, the criteria are general because there are no other criteria for the top level to use, and they are left general so that lower levels of management and staff can break the general criteria down and define more precise criteria. It is essential that staff who will carry out the finer delineations of objectives be given the opportunity to define and refine the criteria and to do so in the way they know best. In other words, staff who are providing a direct service must be given an opportunity to do the job as they see fit, given the limits of top management. This is staff responsibility, and the staff should be considered specialists in this area.

An individual within an organization can meet and/or be responsible for only a certain level and number of objectives if he is to do his job effectively. If an objective requires a number of staff for implementation and is complex because of a large work scope, the overall objective by top management will probably contain general measures. In developing measures for objectives, however, top management must set some numeric criteria for overall performance and cost. The measures must reflect reality, and management should always use hard data when they are available for the purpose (for example, 20 drop-outs, 32 competencies per week, 31 planning seminars, $20,000 per year). If hard data are not available, operational staff should be involved in determining the criteria, though top management must make the final decisions. If they are determined, critical simulation or even research data can be used to improve the decision.

Organizational Levels

Depending upon the size of an organization, there are numerous levels between top management and operational staff. It is often helpful to clarify what constitutes those levels and to delineate the basic functions that are performed within them. There are several ways of categorizing organizational levels in which objectives are delineated. The levels are defined differently by various authors, but terminology and classification are not as important as understanding that the levels are definable.

A small service organization might be made up of several levels, whereas a complex organization might contain multiple levels. Generally, the top level, or the strategic level, is composed of top management. Such members as the superintendent, assistant superintendent, directors, executive secretaries, and commissioners are included. The board of directors or the chairman of the board is also sometimes included. It is the task of this group to review the overall consumer need and to develop strategic service objectives that will meet consumer need. In large service systems, objectives will certainly contain some general criteria.

The next level on which objectives are delineated is called the administrative level. Here middle managers, associate and assistant directors, supervisors, department heads, principals, and deputy commissioners begin the task of analyzing strategic objectives and delineating administrative objectives. Here too they make a more detailed study of the consumer population and refine criteria. At the administrative level there can be a degree of generality, especially when numerous staff are involved and the work scope is complex.

The ultimate service delivery level can be called the "operational level." Here services are provided directly to the consumer population. Members include teachers, counselors, therapists, nurses, house parents, social workers, and attendants. As at higher levels, the operational staff must analyze higher-level objectives and delineate operational objectives. Again, consumer needs must be analyzed at the more detailed level. At this level, much of the general nature of the objectives is eliminated, but even there, the objectives can be general if the consumer is to have the opportunity to reach an objective in his own way.

Here let us refer to Figure 3-2, which is the result of analysis and the breakdown of Figure 3-1. In Figure 3-1 an objective is required for matching the job skill level. This means that, by the time the operational level objectives were written, middle management would need to determine the companies and jobs for placement and operational staff would need to determine the skill level required for success. In this example, an assembly job in a small electronics firm was selected for a work release placement. The required skill level was to place transistors flush on a printed-circuit board at the rate of 40 per hour. The operational staff projected that it could test six per week over a two-week period of time and stay within the placement constraints. They also concluded that the

Figure 3-2. Operational-level measurable objective for testing job placement skills.

MEASURABLE OBJECTIVE				
I.D.	With This	Do This	This Well	Product	This Many
1.8	1. Job performance assembly standards. 2. Work simulator. 3. After three days' practice. 4. Four-hour testing session.	Test individual inmate's assembly against assembly standards.	1. Check if each transistor is placed flush. 2. Rate of 40 per hour. 3. Score by number not flush and deviation from hourly rate.	1 test	6 per week over two weeks.

best method of testing was in a simulator, that three days of practice were needed, and that three four-hour testing sessions should be used.

Defining objectives is perhaps no more important than the other steps in defining the system, but it is one of the most difficult and time-consuming ones. Not all objectives or criteria can be included in any one plan; only those that are *realistic* and *functional* should be included. One mistake is to be unreasonably precise; there are those who lose sleep because they cannot reach the ultimate detail. Too much detail can produce inefficiency because it overwhelms the system; yet if there is too little detail, ambiguity and questions concerning the true effects result. After a human service system works with objectives over a period of time, those within will select the level of objectives that provides the best balance of effectiveness and efficiency.

Two final problems will certainly arise in developing measurable objectives; they are the familiar ones of (1) common standards and (2) "apples and oranges." Developing a common, overall standard is not essential. Each component of the human service system can develop its individual standard as long as it is within the limits required by top management. For example, teachers often complain that, if they are evaluated on the basis of student performance, the teachers in ghetto schools will be penalized. That is a false assumption, for a standard can be developed for each school, each classroom, or each student.

When someone is determining how to add up products across or up through various organizational levels, the usual objection is that "you can't mix apples and oranges." There is nothing wrong with mixing apples and oranges if you are counting fruit. The man who runs the fruit market is as concerned with how much fruit he sells as he is with how much of one kind of fruit. Even a particular kind of fruit is not uniformly the same. Similarly, a superintendent is concerned with the total number of school graduates, but he will also consider the types of degrees acquired. The teacher should be concerned with the overall knowledge and skills acquired by students, but that does not mean he will not consider individual student gains. Even an individual student will be concerned with the overall knowledge and skill he acquires, but he may want to consider a given area separately.

It is only natural that some areas of instruction are more difficult and time-consuming than others. Although we must recognize that and deal with it individually, there is no reason why apples and oranges, or pears and bananas, or even carrots and corn, cannot be added together so long as they are properly classified and used accordingly. We can and undoubtedly will look at the data collectively or singly. The secret is in determining what must be measured at what level and by what standards. A standard for all fruit, a standard for apples, a standard for Jonathan apples, a standard for large Jonathan apples—all are means of measuring fruit. Could not a similar principle be used in human service?

Modeling the Human Service System

The coordinator (a person who is to bring two components of a human service or two human services together) is probably the least effective individual in the entire field. This person typically has numerous responsibilities, yet little authority and no real power. Even when the coordinator can develop a power base, the complex relations between the system and system components are often overwhelming and impossible to deal with. The coordinator's position is typically the creation of one or more managers who believe that there should be a higher degree of cooperation and that a cure-all coordinator will provide it. It is obvious, however, that the various systems or system components typically will not become autonomous simply with the aid of the coordinator. Each has its own group interests and functions to perform. Each has little to do with its counterparts unless there is some direct relation that sustains a common interest.

How can the problem be resolved? Perhaps the coordinator should be replaced by a systems advocate who has the authority to insure that the systems or system components integrate harmoniously in a management control system. That is not possible, however, unless the objectives and relations of component objectives are defined. Defining the components and their relations is possible with a tool that can be used to graphically and/or physically identify the human service system or model it. Systems blueprinting techniques can be used for this purpose much in the same way that an architect uses a blueprint to model a building's components and their relations.

What is a model? We often hear about an educational model, a correctional model, or a welfare model, but when several parties try to reach agreement on what a model is, a great deal of disagreement usually results. There is also controversy over the components of a model. Is a model composed of concepts and principles or of real-life objects? Such questions are often addressed, but answers have not been forthcoming in the field of human services. If human service managers were to follow the examples of other professions, they could certainly answer the questions quickly; for it is true that when other professions have developed methods of producing precise models, their technical capability has been enhanced significantly.

Laurence J. Peter is known for his three popular books, including the well-known *Peter Principle*, but few people know that he is the author of four volumes on teacher competency and accountability. Dr. Peter worked with autistic children for almost twenty years in conceptualizing an innovative model. At one point, he told the author, he thought he knew everything about his model; but when he retained a systems analyst to display the model graphically, he found that he really knew a great deal less about it than he thought. He spent a number of frustrating days analyzing, challenging, defining, redesigning, and eliminating various components of his model. He also spent a good bit of time determining how components would fit together while sequencing and resequencing them. His experience is not unusual. When managers use modeling techniques for the first time, they are often discouraged by how little they know about their organizational models, but they are often encouraged and fascinated with their new discoveries.

What is a model? It is a form, a shape, or a design with numerous internal shapes and designs that are related in some fashion. Models can be illustrated with shapes and lines, but they are often refined with both linguistic and numeric symbols. Various techniques with various rules can be used to develop and illustrate models in the same way that a draftsman uses various techniques for different purposes.

Models can be used to illustrate concepts and principles just as easily as they can be used to display real things or actual service operations. To develop the final graphic model, several graphic models at various stages will probably be used, including (1) the concept model, (2) the program model, and (3) the operational or procedural model. In fact, there is a sequence of model-building techniques that can be used to correspond with the development of the total model. As concepts and principles are analyzed, subsequent goals and objectives can be defined and broken down into minute objectives, all of which can be graphically displayed. Criteria within the objectives and the relations of the objectives are certainly integral parts of the complete graphic model.

The second step is to develop a real-life test model based on the graphic model. The test model is a smaller version of the final model to be produced; it is analogous to a scaled-down model of a bridge or automobile. Perhaps only one component of the model might be tested at a time (such as a single classroom used to model competency-based instruction of a single class in one subject).

The final step is to produce real-life models of programs on a large scale. By this time, most problems should be identified and accommodated by modification, although that process is continuous. Models are not cast in concrete; they must be modified to meet new needs or to correct deficiencies. For that matter, there are no steam engines, airplanes, automobiles, toasters, or space modules that are exactly like the prototypes. When modifications were needed, they were made; and when modifications are needed in human services, they must be made.

Model-Building Techniques

The balance of the chapter describes various techniques that can be used to illustrate the human service system graphically. The system can be represented, like a building on a blueprint, and analyzed. Overlap and deficits can be detected, and the solutions for improving relations and flow of services can be formulated. Graphic models cost little to produce, and simulations made graphically are far less costly than implementing change within the service system without understanding its full impact. Many difficulties can be eliminated in the model alone. When the final model is developed, it will indeed serve as the blueprint for implementing change or managing performance. Managers and staff will then have a mechanism that graphically illustrates what they are to do and how they are to relate to others.

One problem in overall human services management is that managers often do not study the total system. Our transportation system is a good example. Railroads, freeways, airlines, and city buses are transportation subsystems, yet no one plans them as part of an overall system. In some cases they compete; in other cases none of them meet consumer need. As a result they are neither coordinated nor autonomous, and an inefficient transportation system exists. In various branches of government there are departments that were designed to supplement one another but do not interact. Some staffs admit that they do not intend to interact with other departments. Might not model-building techniques be used to develop human service systems jointly so that the systems work to accomplish common goals? Could not models serve as the basis for communicating with others and holding various parties accountable?

Most often, every planner or individual who attempts to reduce the chaos of a human service system reverts to some form of graphic display. The problem is that these graphic displays are often lacking in meaning to anyone but those who developed them. Just as language-modeling techniques have a series of rules that must be used with a particular model-building technique, so human service models must follow commonly understood guidelines. Certain model-building techniques are applicable for some purposes and others are not. Some common model-building techniques will be described at this point, and brief statements concerning their utility will be made.

Block diagramming

Block diagramming is the most simple type of model building. Various components are identified and sequenced together graphically by using cells or blocks as

Figure 3-3. Block diagram of training steps in a vocational training program.

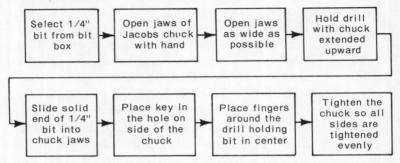

in Figure 3-3. The block diagramming technique is easily used; the rules are simply to define a series of concepts, principles, objectives, or tasks and sequence them in the proper order. Cells made up of rectangles and descriptive legends or symbols identify the various components, and arrows show the sequence.

The problem is that block diagramming can show only one dimension or sequence of components whereas numerous dimensions are often needed to illustrate a complex human service system. The technique does provide a means of illustrating information in a format that is common to most groups who have little working knowledge of models.

Latticing

Latticing is best described as an analytical model-building tool; it is illustrated in Figure 3-4. The lattice is constructed by placing a block or cell containing the major outcome on the top right-hand corner of the paper. As the major outcome is analyzed, components are re-

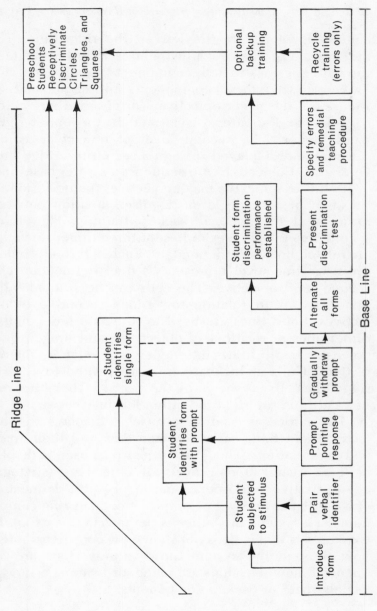

Figure 3-4. Lattice of a basic form discrimination program for nursery school children.

corded down and to the left on the ridge line. The hierarchical sequence is illustrated from left to right. As the lattice is constructed, components are analyzed and broken down into subcomponents and sequenced. In Figure 3-4 the major objective, "discriminating circles, triangles, and squares," is located in the upper right-hand corner. The second level of objectives is delineated and displayed in sequences on the ridge line. Operational objectives are sequenced on the base line.

In this example the major objectives include (1) identification of a single form, (2) discrimination between forms, and (3) optional backup training. The three second-level objectives represent three dimensions that are related but also independent. Each of the cells below the ridge line level represents a finer delineation of a second-level objective. The cells can be studied independently or in relation to various second-level objectives. Solid lines are used to illustrate independent dimensions or relations of objectives, and broken lines are used to illustrate interdependent relations of objectives. Cells at the base line are related to specific ridge line cells (as shown by the arrows). The lattice can be read from top right to bottom left or vice versa.

The lattice is useful because it displays the objectives and their various dimensions and their inter- and intrarelations. The lattice can also be used to display various organizational levels of objectives (strategic, administrative, and operational levels, or a delineation of a particular level). For purposes of analyzing components of a system, the lattice is perhaps the best tool. Its weakness is that is does not show how consumers might flow through the system, how various steps are sequenced, how decisions are made, or when and how to use alternate or backup components.

The algorithm

The algorithm is perhaps the most commonly used model-building technique. It has been used largely in computer work to reduce complex language problems that needed to be solved in order for man to communicate with machines. Algorithms are also used to develop computer programs, define human service systems, and develop subsystems within existing human service systems. They are not used to the extent that they might be to plan and evaluate human services.

As in models discussed previously, various functions or systems components are identified and illustrated by rectangles or cells and flow is indicated by lines with arrows that lead from one component to another. Algorithms also involve several major techniques that differ. First, they make use of symbols to identify points where decisions are made and show results of decision. Second, they make use of various identifiers such as "start," "stop," "go to," and "input."

Figure 3-5 is an algorithm of a general screening, diagnosis, and evaluation (D&E) process. Decision points are used to determine the extent to which the consumer will be examined both before and after the general examination. Start and stop cells identify the points at which the process begins and ends. Of course, this general model would be broken down into numerous steps at the operational level if the examination process included a large number of tests and personnel. Not only would functions be added but decision points would be added as well.

The advantage of the general algorithm model is utility in illustrating multiple paths and flow, displaying alternate paths, specifying decision points and criteria for

Figure 3-5. Algorithm illustrating general screening, diagnosis, and evaluation process.

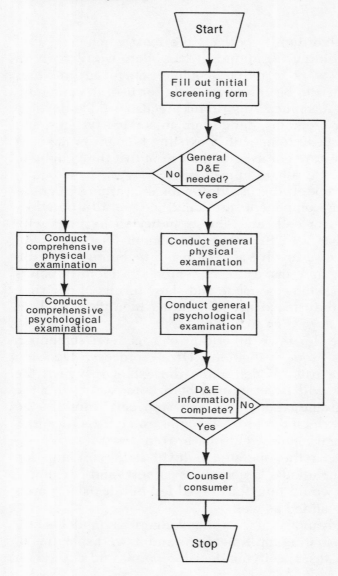

determining when to use paths, and providing general identifiers. Algorithmic model-building techniques are typically developed through a synthetic process, and therein lies a weakness. Analysis of the various systems being illustrated must be performed and components must be identified before they are synthesized into the model. A useful approach is to use a lattice for analysis and the algorithm for synthesis. Because the algorithmic technique is so widely used, it is familiar to most people.

A particular type of algorithmic model-building technique that has afforded good utility is called LOGOS (see Figure 3-6). The technique was developed by Henry Silverman, who describes his model-building

Figure 3-6. LOGOS model for improving human service systems.

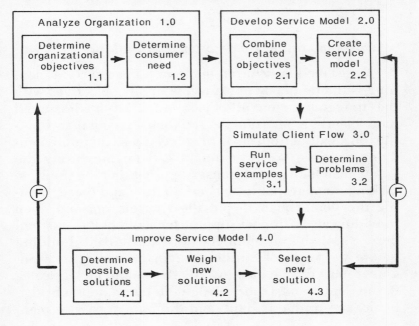

process as being both analytic and synthetic. He has coined the term "anasynthesis" for the process. LOGOS is perhaps the best model-building technique for defining boundaries and various levels within the system. First, boundaries for the system and various subsystems are identified and graphically illustrated. The functions within the subsystems are then identified and defined. Finally, the relations are identified and flow between the various subsystems and components is illustrated. LOGOS presents a difficulty in that, although it identifies components and the flow between them, its graphics can become confusing as numerous relations are defined. An additional sheet describing decisions and relations for flow and the various alternative functions is thus needed when the model is developed in detail.

Implementation time–cost model building

A mistake that is often made in human service planning is the tendency of managers to mix objectives with the implementation of objectives. That is illustrated more clearly in an example in which a young man's putting on a pair of trousers is the objective. The implementation process, however, might call for measuring the young man for a pair of trousers, purchasing the trousers, making them available at a certain time and place, training the young man to put the trousers on, and even providing an additional support such as a belt or suspenders. Similarly, an architect must design the building before the work of building begins, the electrical engineer must design electric circuitry before he fabricates it, the dentist must fabricate a model for a dental bridge before the bridge is built, and the human service manager must develop a model of the human service system before he determines how to implement or modify the system. The goal of the program or service system has been illustrated in preceding model-building techniques. At this point, models that can be used to *implement* the service system will be discussed.

Once the program or service system model is developed, it can be analyzed and various functions that will need to be performed for implementation can be identified. Figure 3-5 serves as an example of the service system. Analysis of the screening, diagnosis, and evaluation model must be made to determine the functions to be performed in implementing the service system. One must assume that the system is nonexistent and that it will be set up in a new or improved center. Analysis of the service system model would lead to the identification of such functions as acquiring planning and evaluation forms, acquiring and preparing staff, and selecting and securing equipment.

Figure 3-7 is an example of an objective or task time model-building technique that can be used for implementation purposes. The chart was developed by Henry L. Gantt at the turn of the century, and it is a tool that is widely used in business today. Functions or objectives to be achieved are listed along the left-hand margin. Estimated time and the beginning and completion dates of objectives are listed across the page. Such other information as names of personnel responsible for achieving the objective, the percent of their time to be spent in achieving the objectives, and even quality and quantity measures within the objectives can be added. The Gantt chart is a simple tool to understand and use; but if the system is complex, other model-building techniques may be needed.

Figure 3-7. Gantt chart for implementing a screening, diagnosis, and evaluation service system.

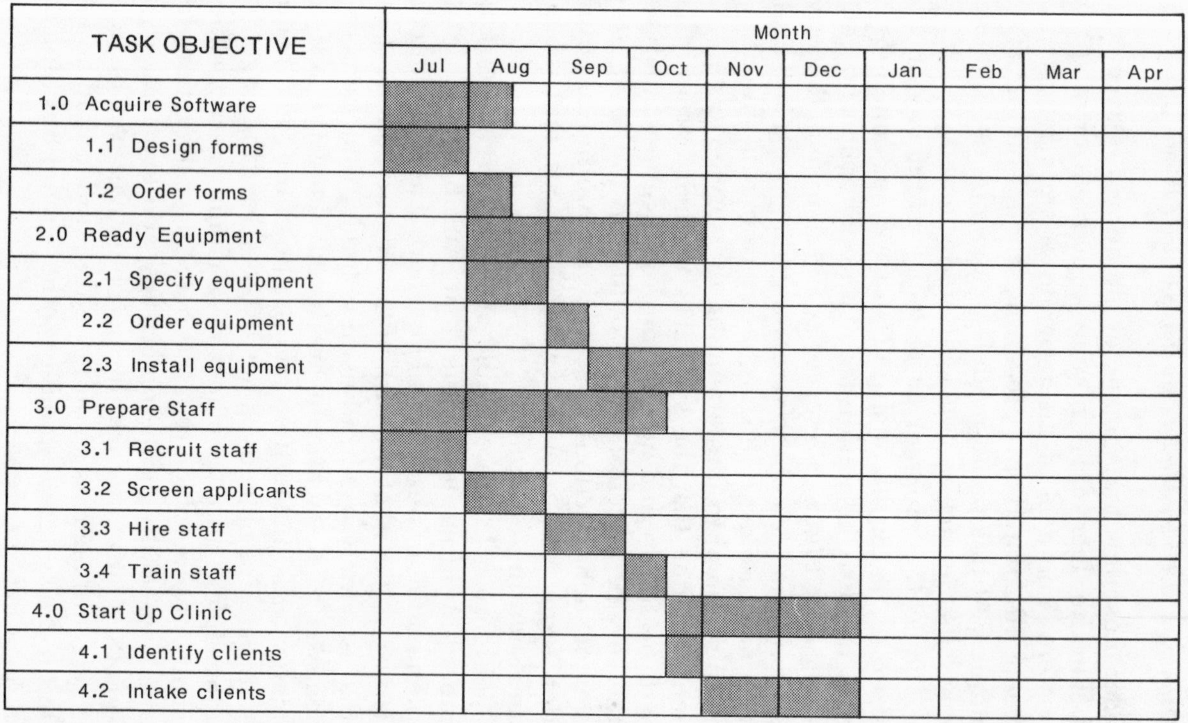

TASK OBJECTIVE	Jul	Aug	Sep	Oct	Nov	Dec	Jan	Feb	Mar	Apr
1.0 Acquire Software	▓	▓								
1.1 Design forms	▓									
1.2 Order forms		▓								
2.0 Ready Equipment		▓	▓	▓						
2.1 Specify equipment		▓								
2.2 Order equipment			▓							
2.3 Install equipment				▓						
3.0 Prepare Staff		▓	▓	▓						
3.1 Recruit staff		▓								
3.2 Screen applicants			▓							
3.3 Hire staff			▓							
3.4 Train staff				▓						
4.0 Start Up Clinic				▓		▓				
4.1 Identify clients				▓		▓				
4.2 Intake clients					▓	▓				

Month

Other model-building techniques that were developed for implementation of objectives over time and for the allocation of cost needed to achieve the objectives are the program evaluation and review technique (PERT) and critical path method (CPM). With these two similar techniques the service system model must be analyzed and the implementation objectives defined. Time and/or cost for achieving the objectives may then be projected.

The final step is to sequence the objectives or objective tasks into a model that illustrates the overall time and/or spending schedule. That is done by putting the various objectives in the order in which they are to be accomplished. When various objectives are ordered, it is typically found that certain objectives or objectives within a task make up an independent sequence that is called a tail. Some tails can be achieved simultaneously; others cannot be started until another tail has been completed. Once the tail inter- and intrarelations have been defined, the tails are sequenced into an overall implementation time and/or cost model.

A model of the PERT/CPM type is developed by laying out a series of arrows, which are tails that separate or join depending upon the inter- and intrarelations. Each arrow or activity represents an objective or task. Circles, or events, are drawn before and after each arrow. Events are the points at which objectives are implemented and completed. Dashed lines with arrows represent communication links in which the activity does not require energy or cost. If the implementation schedule in Figure 3-7 were converted to a PERT/CPM model, it would be similar to the one in Figure 3-8. Once the model is drawn, duration time is recorded above the activity lines. Then one duration time is added to another, be-

Figure 3-8. PERT/CPM implementation model for a screening, diagnosis, and evaluation service system.

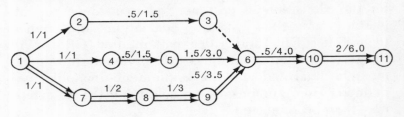

I.D.	Events	Task Objective	Duration in Months	Earliest Start	Earliest Comp	Latest Start	Latest Comp	Slack Time
1.1	1-2	Design forms	1.0	1.0	1.0	1.5	1.5	2.0
1.2	2-3	Order forms	.5	2.0	1.5	3.0	3.5	2.0
2.1	1-4	Specify equipment	1.0	1.0	1.0	.5	1.0	.5
2.2	4-5	Order equipment	.5	1.0	1.5	1.5	2.0	.5
2.3	5-6	Install equipment	1.5	1.5	3.0	2.0	3.5	.5
3.1	1-7	Recruit staff	1.0	1.0	1.0	1.0	1.0	0
3.2	7-8	Screen applicants	1.0	2.0	2.0	2.0	2.0	0
3.3	8-9	Hire staff	1.0	3.0	3.0	3.0	3.0	0
3.4	9-6	Train staff	.5	3.0	3.5	3.0	3.5	0
4.1	6-10	Identify clients	.5	3.5	4.0	3.5	4.0	0
4.2	10-11	Intake clients	2.0	4.0	6.0	4.0	6.0	0

ginning at the left, and cumulative duration time is calculated and recorded below the duration time for an activity. The data are also recorded and/or calculated on a corresponding PERT/CPM matrix together with the late and early starting times. As with the Gantt chart, objective tasks are determined and an identification number is assigned. If additional criteria for objectives are needed, measurable objectives forms can be supplemented.

The critical path

Tails such as 1.1–1.2, 2.1–2.3, 3.1–3.4, and 4.1–4.2 will take up varying amounts of time. Therefore, when adding up the cumulative duration time across various tails, time must always be added onto the tail with the longest amount of cumulative time (tail 3.1–3.4 to tail 4.1–4.2). Because there are varying amounts of time within tails, slack time is created. To determine slack time, a critical path (the longest cumulative time for the overall model) is calculated. The critical path is designated with a double arrow and denotes the longest possible time that it will take to complete all objective tasks. Calculations derived from this procedure denote the earliest possible time in which objective tasks can be initiated and completed.

To calculate slack time, duration time is subtracted from the final cumulative total, starting on the right. A reversal procedure is used, by which the latest possible time that objective tasks can be started and completed is determined. Calculations for the critical path always remain the same for the earliest or latest start and completion dates.

In the event that cost-implementation models are to be used, costs are projected and then sequenced by using the time-implementation model. Costs for individual objectives and objective tasks are entered above the appropriate activity arrows. Cumulative costs are determined by adding the cost of each objective task in the sequence that the tasks occur. In this instance, cumulative totals for various tails are added at the points where they are combined.

The value of PERT/CPM is that it can be used to model complex implementation schedules. It is also easily adapted to computer programs; and as real data are entered into the program, the effects of any deviation can be programmed to depict new start-stop dates. The disadvantage is that the technique is difficult to use for simple short-term implementation schedules.

Conclusion

Some of the techniques that can be used to model human service systems have been summarized and illustrated. The intent has simply been to acquaint the reader with them. Numerous texts on how to build models are available. Managers should choose the model-building techniques or combinations of techniques that best meet their needs. Planners or systems analysts can often be employed to develop the initial models, and operational staff can be trained to use the techniques in their planning.

4

Determining human need and planning for need

A business that fails to determine the needs of consumers with a certain degree of precision or fails to create markets for its products will soon go bankrupt. For the most part, that is not true of human service systems. In conducting strategic planning in education, for example, the most common method used to determine need is to project enrollment through "cohort survival." This may yield data on the probable number of students who will enter public schools, and therefore the need for space, but not on the need for knowledge or skill or other lifestyle requirements.

What should be determined? The number of classrooms or the programs that will lead to some educational outcome? Most individuals would probably say both. Most consumers of educational services are satisfied with a service that includes all school-age persons; that is the basic requirement for satisfying students and parents. A business could never satisfy its consumers that way. Its foremost concern must be with products or outputs, not merely with providing room for the process. Successful businesses spend a great deal of money analyzing markets in order to determine products that consumers will purchase. Most schools spend little, if any, money in that area, and the responsibility for determining need usually resides with the teacher once the child enters school.

That does not deny that the teacher can provide a needed link in determining need; it merely states the fact that most school administrators are less concerned with student need than they are with providing the process and a place for the process to take place. This phenomenon is true not only of education but also of the majority of human services. One of the ways to improve the process is to first define the human service products and then determine the process.

Businesses are not always accurate or without fault. Because of the profit motive, they often provide consumers with what they want, *not with what they need.* For example, over the past two decades, automobile manufacturers have developed high-performance, luxury automobiles that use fuel at a monstrous rate. Some engines in automobiles built for use on regular highways were developed to exceed speeds of 140 miles per hour, and they consume fuel at a rate of more than one gallon per 10 miles. Actually, mass production of such high-performance engines should have been questioned even before the energy crisis; for there are few instances when high-performance engines can be efficiently used in a "family car."

In the short run, the automobile manufacturers made high profits by selling consumers what they wanted or what the manufacturers convinced them they wanted. As a result, consumers and manufacturers ultimately suffered during the energy crisis. Human service, like business and industry, occasionally provides consumers with what they want rather than with what they need. Thus, needs assessment can be invalid if it reflects unrealistic desire rather than actual need.

Human services consumers are often satisfied with token services. Guardians, parents, or relatives are frequently relieved that a son, daughter, mother, father, brother, sister, or grandparent has a place to go for services, even if the services are substandard and dehumanizing. When a family reaches the point at which they can no longer tolerate a member with mental illness, mental retardation, a severe medical disorder, epilepsy, or other disability, they send the member to whatever residential service facility is available.

Often there are no alternatives, and the family members are placed in dehumanizing and restrictive environments. If alternatives (support services) were made available, it could be that the individual would be cared for in his normal home and that costly institutionalization would not be required. But when managers of human services do not question human need, services will be provided in the same manner over and over again. To the majority of recipients of services who cannot speak for themselves, many years or the final years of their lives are spent in sterile, inhumane environments where long hours of boredom fill the day.

Many people are concerned about such conditions. A whole new legal movement has been created by advocates, parents, and consumers themselves. Litigation can be found at all levels—in state courts, federal district courts, various appellate courts, and the Supreme Court. Many of the initial landmark cases are still pending, and litigation in new areas continues to increase. There is a general feeling that the cost of litigation (in terms of dollars and hardships) is questionable in view of the actual gains. The cost is hard to perceive, however, for the consumers who are not receiving services that meet their needs and who believe they are entitled to such services.

Donaldson v. O'Connor is an example of a landmark court case that was brought about because treatment was not thought to be based on need. Donaldson, the plaintiff, brought suit against O'Connor, a human service administrator. Donaldson was a client who could not obtain a release from an institution even though it was determined that he would not do damage to himself or others. On several occasions people in the community attempted to obtain a release for him. The release was denied, and eventually Donaldson brought suit against O'Connor, the superintendent of the institution. In the lower court, Donaldson was awarded $38,000. The principles established were that the client had not received the kinds of services that met his need—in fact, he had been confined to a service environment against his will. This case was later appealed to the Supreme Court, which sent it back to a court of appeals. As with most legal actions of this type, there is serious question if anyone won.

Lawsuits, or possible lawsuits, have become reality for today's human service administrator. Actions are based on the right to equal educational opportunity, the right to community services, the right to treatment in less restrictive environments, the right to be free of involuntary servitude, the right to be free from unconstitutional practices, and other issues.

There is a common pattern in human services: the services are provided as a process that is taken for granted. Although much lip service is paid to it, consumer need is not often considered. Even when consumers provide input or are moved to ask that the system be improved, they often do not know what to ask for. Too often, little if any money is expended on determining needs and planning innovations that will meet need and/or reduce cost. Universities do little to educate professionals in conducting needs assessment, nor do managers in the service systems reinforce staff or managers for carrying it out. If needs assessment is made, the frequent result is massive data that cannot be interpreted or frustration due to lack of instruments, techniques, time, and patience.

As indicated, the judicial branch of government is increasingly being asked to solve problems resulting from service systems that are poor performers or that do not meet need. But that branch of government was not intended to solve such problems as bussing, the right to treatment, and the right to the least restrictive living alternative. It appears that legislative and executive branches have become encumbered, and layers of bureaucracy compound the problem. Drucker describes the overall problem:

> Yet evidence for performance in service institutions is not impressive, let alone overwhelming. Schools, hospitals, and universities are all big today beyond the imagination of an earlier generation. Yet everywhere they are in crisis. A generation or two ago their performance was taken for granted. Today they are being attacked on all sides for lack of performance.

> Services which the nineteenth century managed with aplomb and apparently with little effort—the postal service, for instance, or the railroads—are deeply in the red, require enormous and growing subsidies, and give poorer services

everywhere. Government agencies, both in national and in
local government, are constantly being reorganized so as to
be more efficient. Yet in every country the citizen complains
even more loudly of bureaucracy in government. What he
means by this complaint is that the government agency is
being run for the convenience of the employer rather than
for contribution and performance. This is mismanagement.

Needs assessment is certainly integral to what
Drucker calls "contribution." If human services are not
to become middle class welfare systems, those within
them must plan systems that will determine true need
and improve the consumer's lifestyle, not maintain, impede, or deteriorate it. This does not mean that educational and human services must be abandoned. Indeed,
they must be examined and improved in light of consumer need. Certain components will need to be eliminated, and others will need to be added. Stufflebeam
uses the term "context evaluation" for what has been
described as needs assessment, and he describes the
process:

> Specifically it defines the relevant environments, identifies
> unmet needs and unused opportunities, and diagnoses the
> problems that prevent needs from being met and oppor-
> tunities from being used. Diagnosis of problems provides an
> essential basis for developing objectives whose achievement
> results in program improvements.

Staff and managers must become innovative and
future-minded. They must be able to dream, concep-
tualize, and find improved answers to meet human
needs. Drucker concurs:

> Objectives of tomorrow? The first thing to do to attain tomor-
> row is always to be sloughing off yesterday. Most plans con-

cern themselves only with the new and additional things that have to be done—new products, new processes, new markets, and so on. But the key in doing something different tomorrow is getting rid of the no-longer-productive, the obsolescent, the obsolete.

Defining Consumer Groups

Many instruments and techniques have been developed for individual consumer assessment, but there are few instruments that can be used to assess consumer need on a systemwide basis, especially at the strategic or top-management level. Strategic needs assessment has a paramount impact on the system, yet operational staff are held more accountable for needs assessment than top managers are. Although emphasis on it is increasing, needs assessment is one of the most underdeveloped areas in the field of human services. Regardless, the manager must find or develop techniques and instruments that can be used to define human need. His first step is to define his consumer group and then define the group's needs. It is important to note that a human service system will typically serve more than one consumer population, and each consumer population must therefore be defined separately.

One method of defining consumer groups is to divide them into the major categories of (1) primary consumers, (2) secondary consumers, and (3) tertiary consumers, as in Figure 4-1. In this instance, a university service and training facility that provided services and training for the developmentally disabled analyzed their consumer population and so categorized the population.

In Figure 4-1 the primary consumer is identified as

Figure 4-I. Consumer identification matrix for identifying related developmental disability consumers and their needs.

Consumer Category	Consumer Population	Need
Primary consumer	Citizens who are developmentally disabled	What can be done to improve their life style?
Secondary consumer	Parents of primary consumers University students Direct service providers Consumer advocates	What means can be used to improve the lifestyle of the primary consumer through secondary consumers?
Tertiary consumer	State developmental disabilities councils Federal developmental disabilities agencies Professional developmental disabilities organizations	What systems work best for improving the lifestyle of the primary consumer?

the ultimate consumer, the one whose lifestyle is to be improved (that is, the person who is developmentally disabled). Secondary consumers are identified as those who have or are being prepared to have direct impact on the primary consumer. They include parents or guardians of primary consumers, university students, direct service providers, and consumer advocates. Tertiary consumers are those who are responsible for the overall service system that provides or purchases services for the primary and secondary consumers. They include state developmental disabilities councils and agencies, federal developmental disabilities agencies, and parent and professional organizations that are affiliated with the developmentally disabled.

All three consumer groups represent potential consumers, but the emphasis in these related consumer groups must always rest on improvement in the primary consumers—the persons who will receive the ultimate product of the service system. If university students or parents are to be trained, courses that train the secondary consumers to improve the lifestyle of the primary consumer must be developed. If local, state, or federal consumers are to be served by designing or implementing new and improved services, the services must also be developed in accordance with the needs of the primary-consumer population.

It is impossible to define consumer need if consumer populations are not first defined. Primary consumers will often be subdivided according to a finer level of need. Needs at each level of management also will be different. For example, the needs of the board of education will be quite different from those of the principal, English teacher, or student. The board will be concerned with the needs of all students; the principal will be concerned with the needs of students in his own school; the teacher will be concerned with the needs of the students in his class; and the student will be concerned with his own needs. But although needs assessment will differ at various levels within the organization, the needs are related. Decisions concerning needs at the strategic levels of management will certainly affect those at the operational level. Correspondingly, needs at the operational level should be communicated to strategic levels.

It is best to analyze the total human service and develop a set of questions that can be used to evaluate consumer need at each level. Figure 4-2 is an example of an evaluation matrix; it illustrates context evaluation questions that could be asked of the members of an educational system. Although the questions at this stage of

Figure 4-2. Comprehensive curriculum evaluation matrix.

Personnel	Need	Validity	Reliability	Cost
Board of Education	Do programs meet student and community need (college prep., vocational, special education, social programs)?	Are programs providing knowledge and skills for postsecondary and community placement?	Are programs producing specified results in all schools?	1. Is cost distributed according to program need? 2. Is cost adequate for program need? 3. Did programs stay within the budget?
Administration	Do courses meet student and community and national manpower needs?	Are courses providing knowledge and skills required for community and postsecondary placement?	Are courses providing entry knowledge and skills for all students?	1. Is cost distributed according to, or adequate for, need? 2. What is cost effectiveness in course areas? 3. How can efficiency be increased without sacrificing effect? 4. Did programs stay within the budget?
Teacher	1. Do courses meet student and manpower needs? 2. Does the comprehensiveness of instructional units meet student need? 3. Do individual instructional course units meet student need?	1. Are courses developing knowledge and skills defined by need and objectives (products)? 2. Do teaching procedures produce most effective and efficient means (process)?	1. Are courses developing specified level of competency in all students? 2. Are teaching procedures as effective and efficient for all students?	1. What is cost effectiveness for courses and course units? 2. How can efficiency be increased for courses and course units without sacrificing effect? 3. Did programs stay within the budget? 4. What resources are needed?

Resource	1. Do resources meet special needs not specified in particular program areas? 2. Do responses meet the backup needs of instructors?	1. Are resources producing knowledge and skill specified in special need and objectives? 2. Are resources producing knowledge and skill specified by teacher (backup)? 3. Are resources meeting individual student need?	1. Do resources affect knowledge and skills stated in objectives in all students?	What is the most effective and efficient method to use for a particular objective?
Student	Do courses meet personal goals?	1. Do courses develop skill and knowledge commensurate with personal goals? 2. Are the courses and content of instruction comprehensive?	1. Is the curriculum working equally well on peers? 2. Is the instructional procedure working equally well on peers?	1. Do the courses take up more time than they should? 2. Do courses develop skill and knowledge with a minimum of frustration?
Parent	Are programs and courses meeting the personal goals of the child?	Are programs and courses developing knowledge and skills specified by the school?	Are programs and courses developing similar levels of knowledge and skills in all students?	How could programs and instruction cost less without sacrificing effectiveness?

development are general, they do illustrate question differences and the relation between and across the various member groups. Note that member groups include the strategic, administrative, and operational levels of management as well as indirect service providers, the student, and the parents.

Definition of Consumer Needs

To define consumer needs is one of the most difficult, and also one of the most important, endeavors of the manager. Persistence, insight, and ingenuity are needed by anyone who undertakes to study a human service system and determine how it can be improved to meet the needs of those it serves. *A means of initiating the process is to challenge the assumptions on which the system is founded.* For example, it is commonly believed that service systems should provide a service and that the more types of service and the higher the distribution of services provided, the better the system.

As should be evident at this point, simply providing services does not improve lifestyle. In fact, there is evidence that certain services in this country have actually impeded and deteriorated lifestyle. That is contrary to the concept of educational and social services, whose goal is or should be to enable all to have a normal productive lifestyle. A more functional approach could be to reduce costly institutions which isolate those with special needs and change the home, educational, or work environment to meet the special needs of human service consumers. That is one concept applicable to those who are mentally ill, retarded, or addicted to drugs or alcohol and to the criminal as well.

Various methods are necessary to habilitate or re-habilitate special-need groups, but the concept of improving lifestyle should remain constant. For example, when an individual commits a crime and is placed in a correctional institution, his lifestyle is drastically changed; and it is questionable whether it is being changed for better or for worse. In that environment, of course, the criminal is no longer free to commit crimes in normal society, but he is often able to commit them in the prison society. In fact, it has been shown that a prison environment typically enables the prisoner to cope with the criminal elements and not the normal elements of society because there is no culturally normal society in prison.

Not coping is the probable reason why the prisoner became a criminal. It would seem, then, that a lifestyle that tends to increase criminal activity is less desirable than one that decreases it and that incarceration is not the total answer to the criminal's needs. In fact, the prison environment often creates a lifestyle less desirable than the one with which the criminal entered. Thus, an intensified criminal lifestyle might be the only one that is being molded and shaped by the human services; for the criminal is locked away because of "society's need" and not the criminal's need. If the criminal is not rehabilitated to a normal lifestyle, both he and society will inevitably lose when he is discharged and continues his criminal activities.

The Effect of Treatment Philosophies

There are numerous philosophies (behavioral, developmental, medical, eclectic, Gestalt, normalization, existentialist, genetic, phenomenological, punitive, humanistic, and benevolent) that affect managers in determining need. Because certain philosophies are ingrained in him, a manager will use them as a foundation for needs assessment. If his philosophies are concerned with medical treatment, he might assess needs as requiring a medical-service delivery model. If his philosophies are developmental or punitive, he might assess clients as needing a developmental or punitive model. And so it is with normalization and other philosophies.

Although some philosophies play an important role in determining human need, others can restrict the process. If arguments concerning philosophies occur, the managers who are the most powerful or the superior debators can determine the philosophy that will be used for needs assessment. Because managers are not trained to merge philosophies in an interdisciplinary fashion, those who developed along certain professional lines can become predominant. Nevertheless, if a manager is to have a philosophy, it should be an eclectic one: he must study all philosophies and utilize those that best meet the needs of the client. Of course, such judgments are often value judgments; but until data are available, the manager can do little more than keep an open mind, challenge and rechallenge philosophies, and continue to collect data to determine the best combination of philosophies that serve to improve consumers' lifestyle.

Improvement in Lifestyle

In order to determine improvement in lifestyle, it is first necessary to define what a normal lifestyle is. The normal lifestyle is composed of many variables. It includes fads, practices, customs, and behaviors that are considered culturally normal in the community and the freedom to practice them. It includes the recognition of civil rights, not the suppression of them. It includes obeying laws and living up to societal responsibilities, not being sheltered from them. It includes normal development according to what is age-appropriate, not impeded development according to what is convenient for society. It includes becoming a productive member of society, not a liability to it. It includes the opportunity to live as others do in a normal community—even though doing so could well require special support services. And although special services might be a component of the lifestyle for a time, they can often be eliminated as the consumer advances in age and career development.

These and other variables are certainly part of a foundation for defining a normal lifestyle and are some of those that are being expanded in order to rate human services as to the degree of normalization that they provide. The Program Analysis of Service Systems (PASS), developed by Wolfensberger and Glenn, is an example that contains some of the above variables as well as others. As such technology is developed, it will be possible to define the normal lifestyle and deviations from it.

If the lifestyles of individuals who are recipients of most service systems were to be analyzed, it would be found that there is no single lifestyle. Typically, numerous lifestyles make up a societal subculture. An example is found in the areas of developmental disabilities, where certain lifestyles are developed or maintained through nursing homes and institutions, others are developed through small community centers, and still others are developed through the recipient's normal home.

The various facilities for developing lifestyles are a result of the service delivery model that is primarily developed from the system's philosophies. If the model is one that merely sustains life, nursing home environments where life is sustained could be the principal determinant of the lifestyle. If the model is one that promotes a normal lifestyle, home environments where normal lifestyles are modeled could be the principal determinant. In essence, if the various models that produce lifestyles were placed on a continuum of alternatives, the manager could analyze the type of service delivery model that his organization provides in relation to the development of a normal lifestyle (see Figure 4-3).

Figure 4-3, the Alternative Life Environments Rating and Tracking system (ALERT), was designed to enable managers to analyze their service delivery system and assess client need. ALERT was developed by analyzing the various general service delivery models that produce lifestyles. Models that are physically and socially segregated from society are placed on the left. They are followed by models that are physically integrated but socially segregated and custodial. Next, the models that are physically and socially integrative but are operated within the facilities of the service system for consumers with involved impairments are categorized. Finally, on the right, services that are operated out of the client's normal home are categorized.

On the left, specific service delivery models included in segregated custodial services are those provided through nursing home care, institutional care, and intensive medical care. Specific models included in

Figure 4-3. ALERT continuum of service models and sample of individuals residing within the models. (Courtesy of KUAF, University of Kansas.)

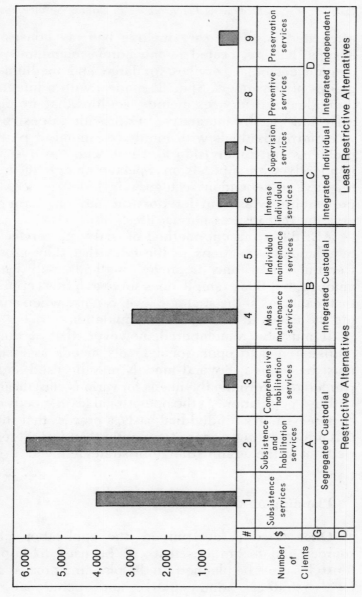

integrated custodial care include halfway houses and hostels that are located in the normal community but operate custodial services for large and medium-size groups of consumers. Specific models within integrated individualized services include facilities that are physically and socially integrative but provide intensive services for individuals with intensive mental or physical problems and supervision for those who can live independently with supervision. Specific models in the integrative independent category include services that prevent lifestyles from deteriorating and long-term preservation that insures normal lifestyles.

ALERT is but one method of analyzing service systems and the relations to lifestyles that they provide. Certainly, new and improved methods will be developed, but this example does serve as a fresh approach that managers at the strategic level can use when analyzing the needs of a large client population.

It must be remembered, however, that at the administrative and operational levels, needs assessment must be refined. Several models may be used and expanded to determine the needs for various classifications within a population. At the operational level, needs must be assessed on an individual basis, a process that should certainly take place more frequently than if it were carried out at the administrative or strategic level.

Planning on the Basis of Need

Once need is determined, the application of resources and techniques that can be used to improve lifestyles must be planned. In the planning process at all levels (strategic, administrative, and operational), pro-

Figure 4-4. General sequence of planning tasks.

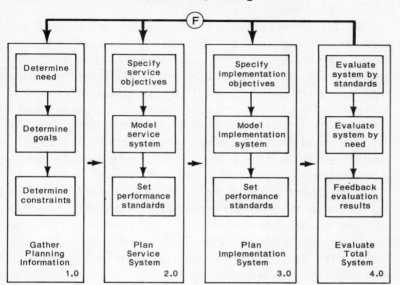

cesses that improve lifestyles must be integrated into the planning. Instruments and techniques that were described in Chapter 3 as useful in defining the human service system can also be used to plan the system. Application of the instruments and techniques should occur in a sequence similar to that shown in Figure 4-4.

First, the planning information must be gathered. The gathering begins with needs assessment and requires the specification of mission, mission profiles, and constraints. At this point, what is needed in the way of overall service models can be planned, but only the components that are needed and can be implemented should be included for the short range. Goals of reducing or eliminating constraints in subsequent years should also be planned at this stage.

Once service goals are set, they must be analyzed and measurable objectives must be determined. At this point, the service system can be modeled and, finally, performance standards can be set. Next, implementation objectives are determined. The implementation system is modeled and performance standards for implementation are set. Note that implementation can include use of real-life models for purposes of simulation. Finally, the implementation system and service system are initiated, operated, evaluated, and improved.

Data from the resulting evaluations must be used by the individuals who are responsible for the various objectives within the system. The information is used to mold and shape the system. Data on both formative and summative schedules are returned, and they are concerned with performance in relation to operational as well as implementation performance standards. Finally, a higher-level evaluation of whether the needs of the clients have actually been met must be made. Again, the issue is not whether the objectives were met, but whether the right objectives were set.

Evaluations, like planning, must be carried out at all levels—strategic, administrative, and operational. If the system is planned, data at the lower levels can be added in an apples-and-oranges fashion to illustrate overall performance, but it will always be necessary to evaluate the individual components to determine what overall performance consists of.

Planning should occur in cycles through a formal process. For example, every six months strategic planning could be conducted and major changes in the organization could be effected. Administrative planning could take place monthly; performance could be analyzed carefully; and intermediate or minor changes could be made in the system when needed. Operational planning could take place daily, and client performance could be evaluated continually and needed changes made immediately. That does not mean there will not be a need for planning and evaluation beyond the scope of the formal cycle. Planning and evaluation should be so conducted as to meet any emerging need in the service system.

A plan is a projection of the system's aspirations, and no one knows to what extent those aspirations will be met. But because plans are projections and because certain environmental or critical incidents will affect plans, it is necessary to reevaluate and replan certain segments as the need dictates. Formal assessment, evaluation, and planning—and interventive evaluation and planning—are needed in all organizations. Emphasis should be placed upon developing a sound plan through the formal process in order to reduce the need for the interventive process.

Conclusion

Needs assessment in human service systems, especially at the strategic level, is something that is difficult to do, something about which little is known, and something about which little is done. Although it is critical for the development of quality service systems, little value is placed on it. The key issue is to assess needs against improvement in the consumer and his lifestyle. Consumers with special needs should be integrated into normal environments, and special systems should be used to maintain consumers in normal environments. Large segregated facilities that restrict consumers from normal environments impede normal development, as do misused or ineffective systems.

Massive service delivery systems based on traditional professional approaches are costly and often ineffective, but they are also firmly established and difficult to change. Managers must be future-oriented, and they must question tradition. They must discover innovative means and tools for meeting needs effectively and efficiently, and they should be reinforced for it. Managers should also plan cyclically in order that needs assessment can be conducted and reevaluations of needs made. Staff should be reinforced for conducting the process, and the needs assessment task must be included as a management objective at all levels.

5

A new approach
to evaluating human
service systems

              "Evaluate our organization?
You bet we're going to do that—next year when we have
time." That New Year's resolution is probably kept less
often than any other. At the end of the fiscal year, one
version or another of it can be heard from nearly all educational and social service managers. And although the
managers are often sincere, they do very little in this
area, and, year after year the resolution is made over
again. In recent years, the federal government has said,
"You *will* evaluate." Among those requiring accountability, however, the federal government should be the first
to integrate effective needs assessment, planning, and
evaluation systems. Even with program planning and
budgeting, peer reviews, and sophisticated data banks,
the basis for most decisions concerning implementation,
continuation, and funding is political. Cost and performance data are considered only secondarily.

    Why are performance data not used in decision mak-
ing? For years human service managers have been using

the terms "cost-effective" and "cost-benefit." Now they are talking about impact, but it is never quite clear what cost-effectiveness, cost-benefit, and impact are or how they can be measured. In some instances, the terms have been misused to create an illusion or to impress a colleague, politician, or consumer. Since most human service systems funding is based on political decisions, the manager is often forced to play a political game if he and his organization are to survive.

Managers of human service systems who have survived have become quite adept at political games. When parents, advocates, or funding sources ask them what they mean by cost-effectiveness, they sometimes respond with anecdotes. "I remember when Toni came here. She was spaced out on drugs—and every boy in town had slept with this poor little 13-year-old girl. Look at her today—about to be discharged from our program." If the manager were a politician, he might put Toni's story in an advertisement or on television. Typically, the public would react by thinking that the program was good and that we need more programs like it. But although the Toni story may be true, it is but one small indication of performance and it provides no information at all about cost. What about the other Tonies, Sharons, Janies, Kathies? What about the program cost that the public must support?

Until human service systems become performance-minded, the political games will be played. That is not to say that the managers who play them are "bad." Politics are a fact of life in business, sports, religion, charities, and even marriage. What should be considered is that there are more games than just the political game to be played in human services. If the service system is to truly meet human needs, we must define the needs, de-

velop effective, efficient, and humane solutions, implement the solutions, and constantly improve them. The
process is indeed complex and cannot be taken for
granted. Managers and staff must learn how to change
their mode of operation, develop new management
skills, modify their work routines, and develop and
utilize the precision to mold and shape the human service system.

What do all these introductory remarks have to do
with evaluation? Everything. First, most management
decisions concerning human services are too often
based on political, and not hard evaluation, data.
Throughout this text numerous examples of why more
performance planning and evaluation instruments and
techniques should be used to improve human service
systems have been provided. It should be evident that
fewer service system decisions should be made politi-
cally and that data resulting from the use of management
information systems should be integrated within the
human service, as well as the political structure, to improve human services.

Measurement Purpose, Importance, and Cost

Once objectives have been determined and the program has been implemented, the next step is to determine to what extent the objectives have been met. This
requires that a measurement system be established. In
developing the measurement system, there are three
questions that must be asked and three decisions that
must be made: (1) What is the purpose of measurement?
(2) Is it important enough to measure? (3) Can the human
service system afford to measure it?

Here is an example of what can happen when those questions are not asked. A subcommittee was appointed to evaluate the effect of monies expended for grants. The grants were used to provide services to the developmentally disabled. One of the grants was submitted and funded solely to purchase a merry-go-round. After the merry-go-round was purchased, the committee reviewed the grant; they began by asking what should be evaluated (client self-awareness or client motor skills to be developed). Because no clear-cut objective had been established in the grant, it was not possible to determine the purpose. The question how important it was to know these things was never asked, and little attention was paid to what evaluation would cost.

Because the issue of purpose was never resolved, a measurement system was not established. General data (number of clients served, health and safety assurances, accounting transactions) were collected anyway, but they probably could not have been used for measurement even if the purpose had been determined. The question of importance was not asked, but the committee believed that it was their duty to evaluate the grant; and they spent a number of long hours trying to determine how to do it. Like the question of importance, the question of cost was never asked, but it was estimated that the cost of submitting the grant, the work of the evaluation committee, and the cost of the data collection and paper processing exceeded the cost of the merry-go-round. Although it might seem that the handling of this event bordered on incompetence, the story does not end there. It was later discovered that the merry-go-round was purchased for a group of mentally retarded adults. The equipment was certainly not age-appropriate and could even be considered dehumanizing.

It might be useful to look at how measurement questions are resolved in other areas. Take an automobile as an example. The question of purpose could be answered in differing ways depending upon the objective. If the objective were to test the strength of a new steel used for a wheel lug, research would be called for. If the purpose were to provide information on general operational performance (fuel capacity, speed, oil pressure, or coolant temperature), evaluation techniques would be required. If the purpose were to determine whether the car was dirty and should be washed, a simple assessment could be made.

Cost is actually asking *what the system can afford.* Certainly some monies must be expended for research, evaluation, and assessment; but if the cost is too high (for instance, if it is more than half of the yearly budget), the system cannot afford the cost of measurement. If cost is too high, either low-priority items must be eliminated and/or the efficiency of existing measurement components must be improved. On the other hand, if few resources are expended and if measurement components are weak or lacking, there is a poor mechanism for evaluating performance. *This is typically the case in human services.*

The decisions of purpose, importance, and cost must be made in human services as well as elsewhere. If a physician were to develop a procedure that would improve open-heart surgery, research instruments and techniques that would produce highly reliable data would undoubtedly be used. The research would be critical for survival and might also be costly; if it were costly, the system might or might not be able to support it. If the physician were to teach interns the techniques needed to perform the new open-heart surgery, the

Figure 5-I. Example of a measurement decision making context for human services.

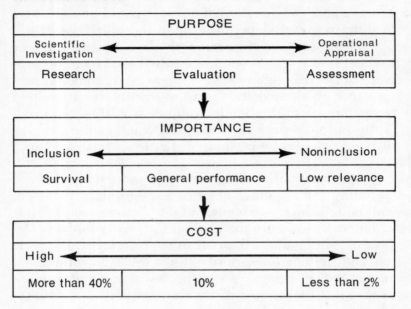

interns should certainly be evaluated on the basis of their skill. Here evaluation techniques would require reliable but perhaps less costly data. Here too it must be decided whether the system could afford the cost of measurement. Finally, the physician might describe the new method to a group of visitors. In that instance, only a simple assessment might be required. If such orientation lectures were not important enough to be measured, there would be no need to resolve the question of cost.

Figure 5-1 is an example of a measurement-decision-making context that can be used for determining purpose, importance, and cost. It is extremely useful to develop such a context when an attempt is made to answer the three major questions concerning measurement. However, it must be remembered that a good deal of common sense should be applied in setting up the measurement system. It is neither possible nor necessary to measure everything, and the task is to measure only that which is necessary, useful, and needed.

Evaluation Centers

If a human service system is defined with measurable objectives and products, and if it is modeled with the techniques discussed in Chapter 3, or with similar techniques, it becomes apparent that there are many points at which evaluation could take place. In preceding discussions in this chapter it has been emphasized that not all components within the service system need to be evaluated, nor is it necessary to use comprehensive research as a measurement technique at the various points. The most common mistake that the manager can make when setting up an evaluation system is to require detailed information about every component in the service system. That can occur when the manager does not understand his service system or when he tries to keep the computer department busy.

An electrical engineer would never consider designing sophisticated electronic equipment without using a schema that included verbal, numeric, and engineering symbols. Also, he would include various testing points for the subsystems. Then, if one of the subsystems were inoperable, it would be possible to test components within that subsystem. The process is similar to the one discussed under the principle of critical indicators and also to the one that the manager must use when defining

Figure 5-2. Example of a system component designated as an evaluation center.

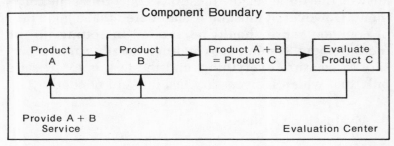

the points at which he will evaluate his human service system.

To specify the points where evaluation is to take place, the boundaries and the components within the boundaries to be evaluated must be determined. If a human service system has been modeled, the complexity of the problem will have been reduced and it will be possible to analyze components of the system and their relations for evaluation purposes (see Figure 5-2). It is not only possible but essential that the design for the evaluation system be included within the service model in a way similar to that of the electrical engineer who builds in test circuitry.

As the evaluation system is being designed, evaluation centers will be specified. An evaluation center is a predetermined point in the service or implementation system where performance data are compared with a performance center. Three major kinds of evaluation centers should be included: product centers, cost centers, and revenue centers. It is possible to designate numerous evaluation centers in the service system at any management level. It is also possible to specify duplicate or multiple evaluation centers at the same point, for example, cost-product, revenue-cost, product-cost-revenue, and product-process centers.

Product centers

Product centers are points at which product performance is evaluated. Each can include one or more system components. Product evaluation can be carried out by using one of two methods. First, product performance can be determined by comparing the quantity or quality of products with the appropriate performance standard. In the second method, both quantity and quality are compared with performance standards as in Chapter 2.

Although performance centers are used to specify the points at which product performance evaluation takes place, they can also be used as the basis for communicating the system product requirements or developing job descriptions. Precise job descriptions can be developed from the product performance standards within the performance center.

Cost centers

Cost centers are points at which cost performance is evaluated. Each can include one or more system components. Evaluation can be carried out by using one of two methods. First, actual costs that are incurred can be compared with the cost performance standards or with cost projections on time-cost models. Second, actual costs that are incurred can be compared with traditional budget categories. A combination of the two is usually desirable to give the manager a complete picture. The first method is used within the management control system, and the second is used within the traditional accounting system. If both are used, they should be merged into a common system to eliminate incompatibility.

Sometimes costs can be traced directly to an input, process, product, or system component and be called direct costs. Sometimes they cannot be traced directly and are called indirect costs. When indirect costs are incurred, they are typically prorated across components or products.

In addition to defining a point at which cost evaluation takes place, cost centers can be used to specify monetary limits for specific or overall components. In essence, a subbudget is allocated to the cost center, and it reflects the total amount projected to be spent at that point. It provides criteria for spending and can be used to control spending behavior.

Revenue centers

Business typically uses the term "profit center" for the point at which profits are made. In human services, profits are considered unseemly. Any profits that are incurred are tucked away in an anonymous fund or directed back to a general fund that usually does nothing for the human service that produced the profit. *It should be recognized that some other human services do make profits.*

Revenue centers are the points at which revenues are obtained. All nonbusiness human services must acquire revenue if they are to exist. If they are to expand, they must engage in behaviors that will generate additional revenues, a behavior that is critical in today's human service systems. As do other evaluation centers, performance standards serve as the criteria that an individual or group of individuals must meet. They can also be used as the basis for a breakeven point below which the service system would be incurring a deficit. Actual revenue that is obtained can be compared with the revenue standards in order to determine performance.

Product, cost, and revenue centers are those that can commonly be used within a human service system, but there are others. There are investment centers in which the objective is to invest retirement funds or unexpended operating funds, and there are purchasing centers which can be used to purchase services from within or outside the system. It is unlikely that the manager of a human service system could develop additional centers. If that is the case, the evaluation center must include some performance standard or criteria that will serve as the basis for evaluation.

Responsibility Centers

The "responsibility center" can be interpreted as being the organizational unit for the performance of which an individual or group of individuals is responsible. Like other performance centers, it can include one or more components found within the system. It differs, however, in that it has no separate performance standards. Therefore, it must include within it one or more of the preceding evaluation centers in order to provide performance standards for which individuals are responsible. If there are no performance standards, it is difficult at best to define just what personnel are responsible for or to evaluate the performance of the organizational unit or personnel charged with responsibility.

Such statements as "I have the responsibility, but no authority," "Those groups can't do anything right," "Why are you out of funds?" and "It's not my responsibility" result when responsibility centers are not used. It is possible to set up effective and efficient evaluation centers, but if no one has the responsibility for performance within them, they are of no more use than if the system did not have them. A responsibility center designates the specific performance criteria that personnel are responsible for and the authority to deal with performance within prescribed boundaries. Evaluation data must be gathered and used by those accountable for the responsibility center in order to mold and shape an organizational unit. A responsibility center should serve as an indicator and major motivator for those who are responsible and will become key components of the management control system to be discussed in Chapter 6.

Responsibility centers can be used throughout the entire service system, and they serve as a means of delegating authority and responsibility. Managers at the strategic level are given specific responsibility centers. They subdivide those centers for the administrative level, and those at the administrative level subdivide them for the operational level. Performance is then reported through the operational level up through the administrative and strategic levels.

General Evaluation Techniques

Numerous techniques can be used to produce data for evaluation purposes. Those thought to be most useful are discussed here. They include impact, cost-effectiveness, performance and cost variance, and performance and cost process evaluations.

Primary impact evaluation

One question that is being asked more frequently of today's human service systems is, "What is the impact of all this?" In reality, impact is effect—the outcome or the end result. Therefore, the program impact should be evaluated on the basis of the outcomes, the end results that were planned or to which the service organization committed itself. Evaluation criteria should be established prior to service program implementation; it is obviously unfair to hold someone accountable for standards developed ad hoc.

But if a program or service is unwilling to specify what impact it has and show how the impact has been obtained, the ad hoc question is not unfair and should be asked continually. In this instance, if impact is to be evaluated, some impact criteria must be selected. Managers must then face the problem of collecting data that can be used to evaluate the impact, since data probably will not have been collected or retained for that purpose. As a result, such ex post facto evaluations typically produce insignificant results.

Impact evaluation for purposes of this discussion is defined by the major effects, end results, or outcomes. The outcomes should and can be measured against performance and cost standards, and they are usually confined to the strategic levels of management. For example, if the ALERT system in Chapter 4 were used to define need and if the service system planned to move 500 clients from the segregated custodial service levels to the integrated individual levels, the impact would be

Figure 5-3. Example of impact evaluation where clients were moved to less restrictive services.

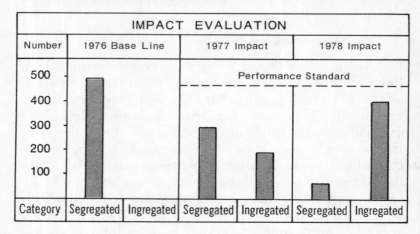

two major levels of improvement in lifestyle for 500 clients. If the movement of a client to the higher-level alternative were defined with a measurable objective and a product designation, a single client movement could be considered a product. If all 500 clients were to be moved within two years, the performance standard could be set at 500. Against that standard, the final impact evaluation could be made (see Figure 5-3).

Another example is that of depicting overall and geographic impact. Figure 5-4 illustrates the clients served by recently implemented mental health resource centers in various state regions. In this instance, the resource centers were used to support clients and provide follow-up in order to prevent commitment or recommitment to mental institutions. Data on clients who received services and who were not committed or recommitted were plotted for the state and various regions. Although total impact, the overall indicator, is the criti-

Figure 5-4. Overall and regional impact evaluation over time.

IMPACT EVALUATION							
Overall Impact				Regional Impact			
Non-committed Clients	1977	1978	1979	Non-committed Clients	1977	1978	1979
900	State Performance Standard			450			
800				400			
700				350			
600				300	Regional Performance Standard		
500				250			
400				200			
300				150			
200				100			
100				50			
0				0			
				Region I			
				Region II			
				Region III			

cal measure, it is also possible to assess contribution and growth of each component in relation to overall impact.

Although the cost of impact is not always included, it can be calculated by determining the difference in cost between two alternatives (such as segregated custodial services and integrated individualized services, as in Figure 5-3). Evaluation at the strategic level should be based not on one year's operation, but on several years' operation.

Implementation costs beyond operating costs should

be included as part of the cost of impact. The efficiency
of the new service should increase after the first year.
Implementation costs can be considered as a one-time
cost or prorated over several years. Objectives defined
on a Gantt chart or objectives and/or costs derived from
implementation of a PERT/CPM model can be used as
cost centers to determine implementation costs.

Primary impact, the major effect, should not be con-
fused with secondary impact. It could be that clients
living within the new alternative or receiving resource
center services would be happier; staff could become
more highly motivated; clients could generate income to
supplement services; state laws or regulations could be
rewritten; and even parents' or guardians' anxiety levels
could be reduced. If such effects do occur but were not
planned, they should be considered secondary impact.
Because secondary impact is usually detected ad hoc, it
is difficult to measure.

Cost effectiveness

To illustrate cost-effectiveness, let us consider the
example of ten social work students who have been
placed at a medical center for their practicum. If effect is
described as two work-ups per student per day, the total
effect for a day is 20 work-ups. If a work-up is defined by
a measurable objective and designated as a product
whenever quality criteria are met, products that meet
criteria can be tabulated each day. Totals reflect the effect for any given day and can be recorded over time (see
Figure 5-5). If the quantity measure in the work-up objective is 20 quality work-ups per day, the standard can
be set at 20 and performance, or the effect, compared
with it.

Figure 5-5. Cost-effectiveness statement of practicum for social work students.

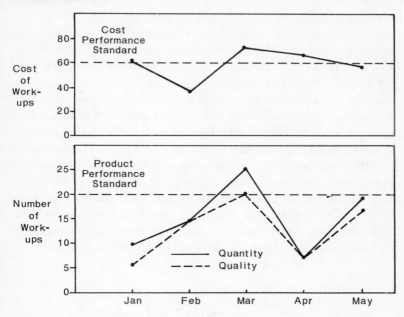

Cost, the other component, includes cost of supplies, equipment and space, trainer, and salaries. Cost could be prorated, but it is best to collect actual cost data and graph it as in Figure 5-5. If cost was budgeted at $60 per day, that can be used as the cost-performance standard. If cost data are plotted above performance data, a cost-effectiveness statement is created and it is possible to analyze both sets of data simultaneously.

Fluctuations occur in both performance and cost behavior, as in all behavior. Sometimes they can be attributed to an identifiable event, and sometimes they can not be. More often than not, they can be produced by a daily event such as a change in process or a change in the resource used. They can be caused by staff motivation, changes in input, or changes in process.

Cost-benefit is another technique that will be discussed chiefly to differentiate it from cost-effectiveness. Cost is defined in dollar units, and benefit is substituted for effect. Benefit is more difficult to define than effect, and its measurement is usually not as easy or as valid. There is also an inherent problem: benefit to whom? Is it to the taxpayer, the client, the client's family, the service system, or even the enemy? Assuming the beneficiary or population has been determined, it next becomes difficult to determine what the benefit actually is or could be. Unless it is possible to define benefit in concrete terms, the technique loses its utility. Cost-benefit is probably best used to make top management projections for purposes of planning or political persuasion.

Performance variances

As described, performance and cost behavior are rarely constant; they are affected by many variables that cannot always be controlled. If a performance standard is used, the product or cost behavior will be more, less, or the same as the performance standards. Differences that are more and less are called variances and are defined with the symbols + for more and − for less. Positive variances are computed by subtracting the performance standard (standard rate) from the performance behavior (actual rate) when performance is above standard. Negative variances are computed by subtracting the performance behavior (actual rate) from the performance standard (standard rate) when performance is below standard.

Figure 5-6 is an example of how variances can be computed when the number of new behaviors acquired by primary consumers is assessed. Behaviors that the consumers acquire for a given month are totaled and charted. If behavioral frequencies are plotted each month, the volume of the behaviors can be evaluated against the performance standard and variances can be calculated.

Performance standards need to be changed periodically—sometimes every year, sometimes every six months, and sometimes monthly, depending on the cir-

Figure 5-6. Monthly total of self-help skills acquired and corresponding variances.

Month	Jan	Feb	Mar	Apr	May	Jun	Total
Standard rate	100	100	100	100	100	100	600
Actual rate	50	100	125	100	150	100	625
Variance	−50	—	+25	—	+50	—	+25

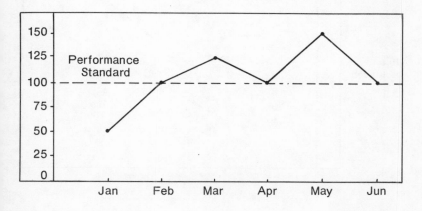

cumstances. If they are changed frequently, a floating performance standard can be used. In this instance, a performance standard is set for each time period in which performance is to be measured. The performance standard for two or more periods might be similar, but infrequently will it be the same.

Figure 5-7 illustrates the use of floating performance standards. In the example, the supervisor and the

Figure 5-7. Variances derived with a floating performance standard.

Month	1	2	3	4	5	6
Floating standard	26	32	36	52	67	70
Actual rate	18	12	21	32	41	52
Variance	−8	−20	−15	−20	−26	−18

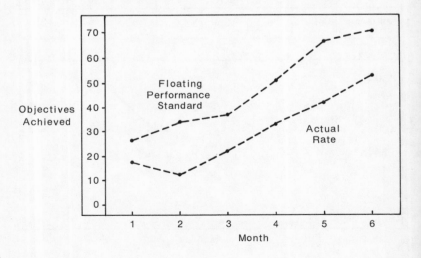

teachers of several public school classes for the gifted set performance standards monthly for objectives being achieved by students in the special classes. The supervisor, the teachers, and the students had determined the objectives of the curriculum prior to implementation. It should be noted that performance standards are minimum standards; sometimes individuals will perform to a performance standard only. If productivity is to be increased, it becomes necessary to adjust the performance standard frequently. Use of a floating standard can eliminate that problem.

Process Evaluation

Before a process evaluation of any type can be made, the product measures must be so defined that various processes or mixes of processes can be used to achieve the highest rate of performance. In educational and other human services, arguments over which process is "better" occur routinely—open or self-contained classroom, corporal punishment or no punishment, special education classes or mainstreaming, Rogerian or eclectic counseling, behavior modification or psychoanalytic procedures. Most research in those areas is inconclusive; there are always several studies that show one process is better than the other. Even when one particular method is found to be most effective, it usually will not work unless the environment and precise procedures are replicated. It is therefore best to define human service products and *experiment with those processes or mixes of processes that will yield the highest performance rate*. This is a continuous procedure.

Figure 5-8 is an example of a process evaluation in

Figure 5-8. Process evaluation using variance to determine the most effective process.

Month	1	2	3	4	5	Tot.	1	2	3	4	5	Tot.
Standard rate	30	30	30	30	30	150	30	30	30	30	30	150
Actual rate	30	20	30	40	40	160	30	20	30	20	10	110
Variance	—	−10	—	+10	+10	+10	—	−10	—	−10	−20	−40
	Process A						Process B					

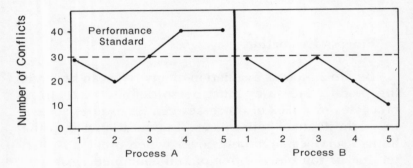

which two distinct processes are used at a counseling center to reduce the number of marital conflicts. As illustrated, over the ten-week period, performance fluctuated above and below the standard. The standard was set at an average number of conflicts of 30 per week, and performance data were compared with it. Process A produced a total variance of +10, and process B produced a total variance of −40. It would seem that process B was more effective.

The same procedure can be used to determine resource mix. Process A could include the use of two individual counseling sessions and one encounter session per week; process B could include one daily self-assessment and two transactional analysis sessions per week. Again, one could yield a higher rate, or it could be that the two would yield a similar performance rate.

Variances can be used to make periodic performance evaluations and to determine the difference between organizational behaviors and performance standards. They can be used for a short-term period, such as a week, or they can be added to determine performance for a longer period, such as six months. If variances are used to evaluate short-term performance, the evaluation is formative; if they are used to evaluate long-term performance, the evaluation is summative.

Process evaluation is sometimes used as cost-benefit evaluation. If one process yields a higher product rate at the standard quality for the same cost or the standard product rate at standard quality for less cost, either one is said to be more cost-beneficial. (This is probably a preferred means of determining cost-benefit, and it avoids weaknesses discussed previously.)

Common Types of Products

Two common types of products can be used to evaluate human services; they are the *standard product* and the *variant product*. They are alike in that both must be defined with objectives and measurable criteria and designated as products. They differ in that standard products will use the same criteria and occur over and over again whereas the criteria for variant products will change. An example of a standard product might be testing fine motor skills. If a specific test were used for the purpose and if several occupational therapists administered the test according to defined criteria, the test could be counted as a standard product each time it was administered. Performance standards could be determined and standard products charted, at which point performance could be evaluated.

Some clients may require more training and treatment than others before a product is attained. The product criteria will remain constant, but the process and resource costs to provide the product may differ. Costs of input and process required until an individual's standard product is provided can be accumulated. If a client billing system is used, the specific amount required to produce a standard product can be shown. In this instance the standard product is charted and other evaluations are used to deal with process and cost.

In overall cost evaluation, at least two methods are available to show the difference in input and process cost: (1) variance distribution, or the range of frequencies of cost, and (2) variance mean, or the mean of the frequencies. Figure 5-9 is an example of how the two are used to evaluate the cost of a standard product of following-directions behavior.

Variant products, on the other hand, are one of a kind. They may occur only once or, if they occur more than once, they may not include the same dimensions. When a service system is implemented, products will often be provided only once (purchasing equipment, training staff, intaking clients) and can be called variant products. In other words, these products vary from others defined in the implementation system.

Then too, it is not always possible to produce a standard product. Even when trucks are manufactured, the units differ. Various accessories are added to the standard model, and cost also is added. In the example of standard human service products, a single test that was administered the same way was defined as a standard product. But because the clients being tested are unique, a complete diagnosis might require the use of several tests, and those tests may not always be the same. In this instance, the product is also a variant product.

Frequencies of variant products can be charted. However, it must be remembered that fruit is being charted—not apples or oranges. In the event that variant products are produced, techniques can be used to measure their variance. The method of Figure 5-8 can be used for both variant and standard products.

Often a variant product can become a standard product. If a variant product is found to occur over and over again, it should be converted to a standard product. For

Figure 5-9. Two methods of evaluating the cost distribution of a standard product.

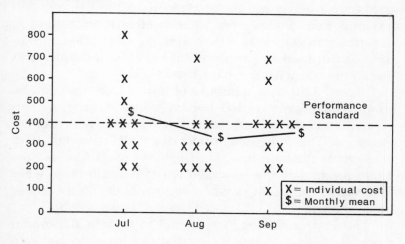

example, it might be found that 25 percent of the clients being tested by the occupational therapist required the same five standard tests. A diagnostic product specifying the five standard tests could be defined as a standard product.

Instruments for Measuring Performance

To be sure, many instruments can be used to measure performance. Throughout this text, charts have been used to display performance data. Such charts are commonly applied to behavioral analysis. And although data from both control and experimental groups can thereby be examined, it is not necessary to use both experimental and control groups. The difficulty and cost of obtaining matched groups can be avoided by using the single-subject or single-organizational design, which is used to compare individual data over time. Performance standards are usually not used; typically a base line of behavioral frequencies over some pretreatment period is the standard. Once the base line is established, treatment is initiated and subsequent behavioral frequencies are compared with the base line.

Figure 5-10 is an example of how a base line can be used. The organizational behavior was defined as service products provided through a community center for the aged. The five-year period from 1967 through 1972 constitutes the base line. During that time, no more than 1,000 products were provided. In 1973 local taxes were first levied, and that is when the product improvement phase began.

The instrument in Figures 5-5 to 5-10 is a common frequency chart. Frequencies that can be added or subtracted are identified on the left along the ordinate. Time intervals (hours, days, weeks, months) are recorded across the bottom, or the abscissa. At each time interval, the frequency with which the behavior occurred is recorded on the corresponding line.

Add-subtract or simple frequency charts are by far the simplest and the most commonly used, but they have a major weakness. They cannot be used effectively to display frequencies with a wide range of variation or to display two or more behaviors that fall within widely diverse frequency ranges. For either purpose, a chart that has a multiply-divide frequency range should be used. In Figure 5-11, two behaviors with widely diverse frequency ranges were used for purposes of illustrating the data. On the bottom, outreach products provided by a

Figure 5-10. Use of base line to measure the effect of a tax levy.

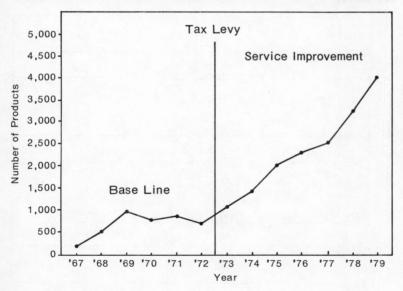

university had a frequency range of from 52 to 790. The data on the top, monthly cost of products, had a frequency range of from $4,050 to $8,100. Although the frequency range 1,000 to 10,000 was adequate for cost data, it was not for the product data and vice versa.

Standardized multiply-divide charts, called semilogarithmic charts or six-cycle charts, were designed for use with wide ranges of frequencies. Six-cycle charts use the standard measurement of frequencies per minute. They are highly applicable to evaluation, especially when wide ranges of frequencies are encountered. Examples are cost-effectiveness statements or behavioral display in which two or more sets of data fall within widely diverse frequency ranges. These charts are more com-

Figure 5-II. Logarithmic chart of monthly outreach products and costs.

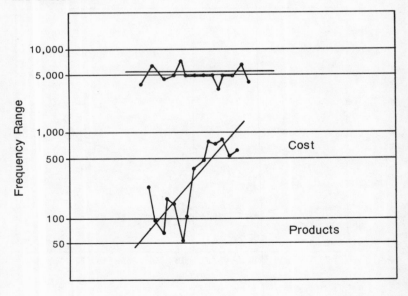

plex, but they are very useful for the problems described above.

Procedures for Evaluating Performance

Almost all the techniques used for behavioral analysis can be used to evaluate organizational or human service behavior. The techniques are highly compatible as long as the product (behavior in behavioral analysis) is defined precisely. Actually, the only difference is that the frequencies (with which behavior is or products are produced) are tabulated and charted for numerous individuals rather than for a single individual. Within the human service system, however, it is quite appropriate to evaluate an individual on the basis of products he has produced or the quality or even the cost of the products.

A frequency is not to be recorded unless the product meets criteria. Legitimate frequencies (those that meet criteria) are plotted on a bar, add-subtract, or multiply-divide graph. Once data are plotted, they are compared with a base line, a performance standard, or data that occurred before or after an event or process. The preceding description summarizes the general procedure for analyzing or evaluating performance. Numerous examples of how the general procedures are used have been provided. In some instances, the procedure was modified to illustrate some particular variation. Now we will discuss and provide examples of additional variations.

Cumulative Frequencies

Cumulative frequencies are plotted almost as often as actual frequencies; Figure 5-12 shows how they are

Figure 5-12. Cumulative frequencies of completed research units.

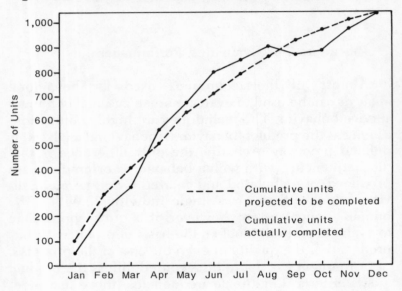

used. In this example, the total number of research modules completed monthly by researchers was plotted. Data from the preceding period or periods are always added to the new period's frequencies. As in previous examples, a performance standard can be used, but here the standard also must be cumulative. Such performance standards are often used to pace organizational behavior. In this instance, over 1,000 modules were to be completed in one year, with the rate decreasing after June.

Multiple products

Sometimes it is necessary to analyze organizational behaviors of various products or product lines in relation

Figure 5-13. Example of product line evaluation.

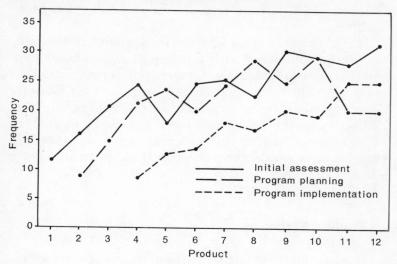

to one another. Figure 5-13 illustrates how several products' frequencies can be charted simultaneously. Initial assessment (product 1) frequencies increased over the year. Program planning (product 2) was not provided until the second month and increased in frequency until the tenth month, when frequencies fell off sharply. Program implementation (product 3) was not provided until the fourth month; and frequencies increased gradually until the tenth month, when they increased sharply.

How are these data used in decision making? In this instance, they could mean that if initial assessment is not being conducted, products could not be provided. Like sales in business, the initial step must be taken. Second, products are provided at different rates according to need, yearly cycles, or perhaps organizational change.

As the change in rate occurs, managers will have to modify resources allocation to meet the need in other product lines.

It is also possible to add the frequencies of the various product lines, as with the apples-and-oranges concept, in order to look at the total output of products. This process would be similar to the one used by General Motors to analyze and evaluate overall automobile production or by the New York Stock Exchange to analyze the volume of trading on the exchange. If this method were used, it would be similar to that found in Figure 5-4.

Product Variances

It was stated earlier that when a variant product occurs repeatedly, it should be converted to a standard product. An example is a class in which 10 students were being taught multiplication. In ten instances, the teacher had to teach the children to multiply three-digit figures (the product). But the teacher also had to teach eight students to keep the rows straight and had to improve the adding skills of three students. The evaluation data were used to analyze the problem because the teacher was not meeting performance standards for multiplication. There were several correctional alternatives. One was adding a product or competency that included addition and keeping rows straight to the product line, or the product that required just multiplication could be maintained, and the teachers could consult with the students' previous teachers to the end of developing a higher performance standard in adding and keeping rows straight.

A-B-A-B design

To determine how well certain processes work, the A-B-A-B design developed for behavioral analysis can be used. Base-line data are plotted for process A; treatment B is initiated and data are plotted; treatment B is stopped, with a temporary return to condition A, and resulting data are plotted. Finally, treatment B is initiated and resulting data are plotted.

Figure 5-14 is an example of an A-B-A-B design in which management attempted to improve the quantity of service products through performance feedback. In the A segment, performance service product data were plotted but they were not shown. In the B segment, service product data were plotted and were displayed each day. In this example, it would probably be concluded that the daily data display or performance feedback increased the quantity of service products.

Figure 5-14. A-B-A-B process design used to show the effect of performance feedback.

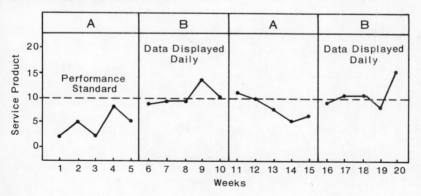

Multiple-base-line design

Another process evaluation tool is the mutliple-base-line design. Like the A-B-A-B design, it was developed for behavioral analysis. It can be used in management by dividing work groups, departments, wards, or schools. In each of the divisions, a process is implemented on a separate day as shown in Figure 5-15. In this example, the monthly program audit was used as the process. It was implemented on ward A in the third month, on ward B in the fifth month, and on ward C in the seventh month. In all instances, product frequencies increased. The data indicate that the process of program

Figure 5-15. Multiple-base-line design illustrating the effect of disclosing the number of training steps acquired by clients.

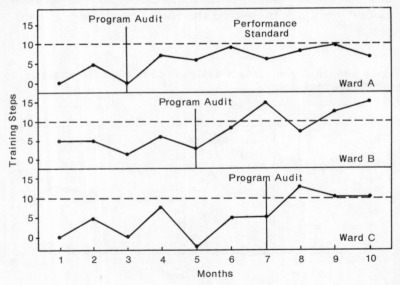

auditing increases performance (training steps) and/or the reporting of it.

Frequency Multipliers and Celerations

When data are analyzed, several common phenomena will occur. First, data will appear to bounce up and down but will stay within a certain range such as 10 to 20 and then at some point change to a completely new frequency range such as 30 to 60. Second, certain trends within the bounce will occur. Overall frequencies may increase, decrease, or remain the same over time.

If standard six-cycle paper is used as the evaluation tool, both phenomena can be measured. The first is called a frequency multiplier, and the second is called a celeration. When a frequency multiplier is to be determined it must be remembered that frequencies multiply as data are recorded upward across a cycle (for example, 10 to 99, 100 to 999, 10,000 to 100,000) and divided as data are recorded downward. (If the technique were used with add-subtract graphs, the term "frequency add-on" might be used.) The frequency multiplier is the distance between frequency 1 and frequency 2. It can be stated in an equation as distance equals frequency 2 over frequency 1, or $D = F^2/F^1$. In Figure 5-16, indirect service products (support products needed to provide direct service products) increased to a new level during June. Indirect products increased from 50 to 400, a frequency multiplier of 8.0.

Celerations are best described as trends in which overall frequencies are found to increase, decrease, or remain constant over time. Related groups of frequencies are used as the basis for plotting celeration lines.

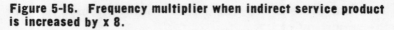

Figure 5-16. Frequency multiplier when indirect service product is increased by x 8.

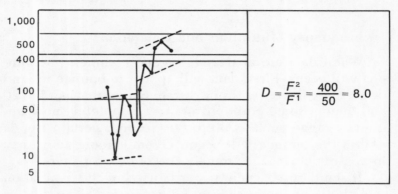

$$D = \frac{F^2}{F^1} = \frac{400}{50} = 8.0$$

Different methods can be used for the purpose (for example, the freehand method, the quarter-intersect method); and once the celeration lines are drawn, the celeration is calculated. The rate is calculated by converting the frequency values into ratios with the formula $C = F^2/F^1$. The frequency found on the celeration line in the middle of the first week is used for F^1, and the frequency found on the celeration line of the second week is used for F^2. In Figure 5-17, the number of products is multiplying at 1.5 over six months, while product cost is increasing at 1.1 over six months. Thus, efficiency is increasing at 1.5/1.1, or 1.3, over a six-month period.

Income Statements

Income statements are used by most businesses on a monthly or yearly basis, but, except for accounting purposes, they are rarely used in human services. Without income statements, however, it is difficult for managers

Figure 5-17. Cost and product celeration.

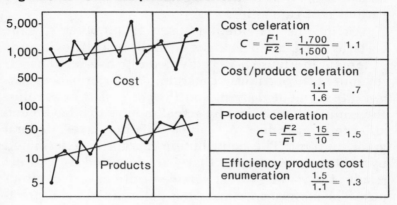

to analyze true costs. When income statements are not used, unrefined methods that produce inaccurate measures are often substituted. For example, if a principal of a school were asked how much it costs to educate the children in the English classes, he might add the teachers' salaries and arrive at a figure of $35,000. On the other hand, if he were asked how much it costs to teach all children in the school, he might use the total budget, which includes more than teachers' salaries. If a manager in a business were asked the cost of operating a department, he could usually provide detailed figures for direct and indirect costs and the various categories that incurred cost. Human services, like businesses, incur costs for providing or producing products that go beyond direct costs. Figure 5-18 is an example of an income statement that might be used by the head of the math department. If the school were concerned about cost, the administration might require that periodic analysis of cost be made to determine where overall efficiency could be improved. If desirable, cost performance standards could be established for any of the various cost categories.

An income statement is used to pinpoint specific costs as well as to analyze overall cost. The income statement in Figure 5-18 is divided into five sections: (1) revenue, (2) contribution margin, (3) performance margin, (4) segment margin, and (5) net deficit or surplus. Revenue is determined by actual monies that have been allocated regardless of source (district taxes, federal grant, tuition). The contribution margin is determined by subtracting the costs that were incurred as a direct result of providing direct service or direct service products. The performance margin is determined by subtracting additional costs that were incurred but were not directly related to service products, and the segment margin is determined by subtracting prorated costs that were committed to the department. The deficit is determined by subtracting the remaining joint costs, such as administrative charges for managing grants or other administrative costs, from the superintendent's office.

It should be noted that some costs can be controlled and others cannot be. For example, the head of a math department can usually control the amount of money spent for materials, textbooks, equipment, or incentives. In some instances, he can even control some service costs. He typically cannot, however, control costs for administrative overhead dispersed by the superintendent. A responsibility center should be used to specify items for which he is responsible and which he can control and those for which he is not responsible and which he cannot control.

If efficiency is to be increased through analysis of the income statement, the analysis should be made jointly

Figure 5-18. Income statement for a school mathematics department, depicting cost breakdown by margins.

Revenue (Yearly Allowance)			$ 90,000
Variable cost			
Materials and textbooks		$ 2,000	
Teacher and teacher aid salaries		35,000	
Equipment rental		3,000	
Teacher incentives		8,000	
			48,000
Contribution margin			$ 42,000
Programmed fixed cost			
Publicity		1,000	
Custodial service		7,000	
Counseling service		1,000	
Nursing service		1,000	
			10,000
Performance margin			$ 32,000
Committed fixed cost			
Secretarial salary	10%	1,000	
Business salary	10%	1,000	
Administrative salary	10%	3,000	
Depreciation		12,000	
			17,000
Segment margin			$ 15,000
Joint fixed cost		8,000	
Joint variable cost		9,000	17,000
Net Deficit			($ −2,000)

with top management. In the math department example, to whom does the deficit problem belong: to the department head who may have purchased costly equipment, to the principal who charged off administrative and numerous support salaries, or to the superintendent who charged excessive overhead and joint costs? If costs that are directly attributable to the products are too high, they should be reduced. On the other hand, if middle-management or other service costs that were charged to the math department are higher than the costs necessary to provide the product, they should be reduced.

An optimum blend of direct and indirect services or overhead must be developed if services are to become efficient. A common problem, however, is that efficiency is the foremost concern. The income statement is introduced last because *efficiency should be considered only along with its effect on performance.* Other techniques that have been discussed earlier must be used in addition to the income statement before or as decisions concerning efficiency are made. Efficiency should never be the sole basis for performance evaluation.

How Is Evaluation Carried Out?

There is a great deal of controversy over who should evaluate human services—those in the service system or someone outside. It would seem that the people who are responsible for product and cost performance could benefit most from evaluation. But if they are not accountable, then outside evaluation will be required. As an analogy, banks keep accurate accounts of their transactions and outside agencies are not used to evaluate performance. Auditors do spot-check a bank's performance, but there is no need for a continuous outside audit. In fact, if the bank did not keep accurate accounts, it probably would not survive long. But whereas controls have been set up for that purpose in banking, there are few, if any, management controls in human services. As a result, little valid internal evaluation is conducted and outside agencies are often favored because there is no alternative.

There should be little argument about how evaluation is to be carried out. The method cannot be determined until the evaluation question has been stated. If an educational service system is to be accredited, evaluated by the level of normalization it provides, or assessed against some universal standard, outside agencies can be used in addition to internal evaluation. External instruments can also be used by internal staff. It is virtually impossible to evaluate performance and cost from the outside. Performance evaluation systems must be built in from the first day. They must be implemented, and they must be used. If management control systems are needed to see that internal evaluation is carried out, they should be used.

Conclusion

Evaluation of human services must be based on common sense. It is ridiculous to evaluate some things, and it is highly critical to evaluate or conduct detailed research on others. The overall system must be analyzed to determine purpose, importance, and cost of evaluation. Responsibility for performance within the related components must be assigned; evaluation and responsibility centers can be used for the purpose. Certain evaluation procedures can be used at various levels within the organization, and they should be selected in accordance with the evaluation questions. Evaluation should generally be conducted as an internal process; but if there is no internal evaluation system, outside evaluation is the only option. Combinations of the two are desirable, but they should be determined by selecting the procedure that answers the evaluation question effectively and economically.

If possible, evaluation instruments that are simple and functional should be used. Those that are based on analysis of behavior are easily adapted to management purposes and afford good utility. Less emphasis should be placed on complicated statistical analysis and more emphasis on practical application if the evaluation system is to work.

The techniques discussed are certainly not innovations. They have been modified for use in the management of human services, and many are used to evaluate and manage primary consumers. A number of other techniques might be added to those discussed, and they can be included in each manager's unique management system; but the manager should exercise care not to add techniques that will not be used.

6

The management
control system:
More than charts
and graphs

People within a human ser-
vice system *are* the system. They have brought about
what exists; they control performance and cost; and they
will shape the future of the system. And although managers can not control the quality, quantity, or cost of each
human service product, they can manage the individuals
who provide the products. This chapter is not concerned
with techniques that can be used to define and evaluate
the human service system. It is concerned with the formal or informal management control system that molds
and shapes the human service system and its products.

There are four basic rules that a manager of a human
service system should follow:

1. Provide service products based upon *true* consumer need.
2. Define objectives, products, and performance
   standards precisely and systematically.
3. Enable staff and managers alike to provide service

products in a way that combines their personal strength and needs with the requirements of the service system.

4. Use a management control system that continually utilizes performance standards and evaluation information and that takes action when and where necessary.

If the management control system is not used, planning, defining, data collecting, evaluation, and feedback can become routine tasks that produce pieces of paper with little or no meaning. Management control systems are effective not because they are sophisticated and highly accurate but because they are simple, functional, and economical—an integral subsystem within the human service system. They are used as the basis for holding staff accountable, making decisions, and taking action.

The Management Control System

A management control system of some type exists in all organizations including the church, the nation, the Olympics, the Mafia, and even Howard's Mexican Restaurant. It is a support system that is used to do what the title implies: control the resources and personnel within the system so that the overall system or organizational objectives are accomplished effectively and efficiently. It is the service that management provides. It can be defined as a subsystem within the human service system, but it is also the guidance core of that system. Like other subsystems, management control systems have products that can be defined, quantified, and evaluated.

Management control systems can be designed only to

control. For example, a police department controls; it does not make the laws or even have a great deal to say about making the laws. More than control is needed in human services. The most effective management control system includes context evaluation and strategic planning as integral components. In that way not only quality and quantity of products are controlled but the system is assured of providing the right product.

Some management control systems actually control, and others simply exist. There are those that can be observed in action and defined and those that are obscure. There are those that lead people and those that push people. There are those that are used to guarantee that consumer needs are met and those that are used only for personal gratification.

Anyone who has worked anywhere for any length of time knows what the management control system is—not what is on the formal table of organization, but the actual regimentation and command. If a person steps out of bounds, the management control system lets him know. To illustrate that, it might be assumed that a warden runs all components within a reformatory. After an inmate spends a short time in the prison, he finds that the warden does not control the society in which he lives, nor do the deputy wardens or even the guards. The inmates control the inner social system; and if the new inmate steps out of bounds, he discovers exactly which inmates are in control. That is not unlike the typical organization, and the successful manager is one who develops a management control system that minimizes informal control and does indeed bring about the molding and shaping process discussed in connection with formative management.

An effective management control system is one that

provides information on how the service system has reacted, is reacting, and will react and one that takes immediate action to mold and shape the system. It does not take unnecessary action based on one critical incident; it takes action on the basis of data. It enables managers to maintain the upper edge by understanding what molds and shapes the service system—or understanding the leaders who do the molding and shaping. It is used to provide the information, guidance, resources, support, reinforcement, and sometimes punishment necessary to meet or exceed performance standards or to manage others. Each management system will certainly be unique. Each individual manager will need to develop his individual management system in a way that meets his or her needs best.

Managing Human Behavior

It might seem that the preceding chapters are concerned with hard scientific principles, instruments, and techniques and that the individuals who operate human service systems are nothing more than tools. On the contrary, the principles, instruments, and techniques are aids to understanding what the overall organization is, what is happening in it, and what it should become. The aids also make it possible for a manager to understand the behavior of many individuals or of one in particular. A manager cannot afford to overlook the individual. That is of paramount importance.

To deal with individuals, a manager must learn to listen to and study others. He must become a leader by helping others and serving as a model. He must give staff new opportunities and give their work meaning and direction. If a manager is concerned about autocratic power, is concerned only about cost and performance, or is too busy to reinforce employees, he has already made his first mistake. He can mold and shape the organization only through the power of others. Therefore, he must determine what stimulates staff or other managers to do their jobs. In effect, he must be a behavioral scientist.

Sometimes managers forget about individual needs because of something as simple as ego. For example, there was a young, energetic administrator who worked hard and eventually became the head of his service organization. He had beautiful social skills; he was creative, bright, self-motivated; he was a superstrategist, an adroit salesman; and he had ambition. It would seem that such a person would have a great future in the overall system, but that did not come to pass because he had a severe ego need. As other administrators within the system achieved gains, he found ways to diminish their achievements because his ego could not tolerate the success of others. For the same reason, he would belittle administrators to whom he was responsible.

Although the administrator ran what seemed to be a model service system, loss of subordinate staff and the resentment of top administrators contained his personal growth and the growth of his services. Eventually he resigned and went elsewhere to start over. Two problems existed. Because of his ego difficulty, he did not allow others to achieve personal needs as a means of molding and shaping services. Second, top administrators did not understand his need. Rather than capitalize on a meaningful consequence, they were offended and fought him, which resulted in the deterioration of services, and everyone lost.

Understanding and using personal need to motivate

staff underlies one of today's most popular management theories. Procedures that are developed from that theory and are used to manage human service systems should be viewed as a powerful management mechanism. They are used in advertising, and they are used effectively in behavioral science. There are consultant organizations that use the theories to motivate employees to improve performance.

Popular Motivation Theory

People respond in one way or another to fulfill their needs. Human needs include what are called primary needs (food, water, elimination of pain), but the primary needs are typically not usable by management. More often, management is concerned with secondary needs (ego gratification, sense of belonging, creative outlets, emotional security, love). It should be noted that each individual has a different set of needs and that the needs are of differing intensity. What is a need for one person is not always a need for another.

Some managers pay little attention to individual needs and make the mistake of thinking that money is the universal motiviator. Money can indeed be a powerful motivator, but it does not *always* work. The schedules with which money is provided to an individual in employment circumstances are not consistent with behavioral principles.

In other words, there may be no real contingency link between work performance and the paycheck. An employee can make all kinds of promises about what he will do if he gets a raise. Managers often believe the promises, give the person a raise, and see nothing more than some token surge in performance. If the manager is to be successful, he must be careful to provide a contingency link between the raise and the promised increase in performance.

People need more than money to take care of their personal needs. Often they will use the work environment to fulfill their remaining needs. Again there may be no contingency link to performance. For example, a secretary may meet her overwhelming need to belong to a group by gossiping and not typing. Unless there is a contingency link, she may end up doing a good bit of gossiping. Even if there were a contingency link involving monetary incentives, it might not be enough to suppress gossiping and motivate typing.

General Context for Motivation

Fran Tarkenton, outstanding NFL quarterback and president of Behavioral Systems Incorporated, a consulting firm specializing in human performance, once discussed motivation. He explained that he used to give pep talks to businesses but found he was only entertaining groups. Motivation, he wrote, was actually tied to performance. If a person was performing high, he was thought to be highly motivated. If he was performing low, he was thought to be unmotivated. According to Tarkenton, a major advancement in motivation occurred in the behavior management field. One aspect of behavior management is providing "meaningful consequences"—one of the most important yet most overlooked factors affecting performance. Providing meaningful consequences" is closely related to fulfilling need.

People act to acquire need fulfillers, and they are reinforced or punished for their action. That is the basis of motivation. Fulfilling need represents positive reinforcement, and withholding something that will fulfill need represents negative reinforcement. Reinforcing a behavior increases the probability that it will occur again. Punishment is sometimes used to decrease or extinguish motivation, but it can act as a motivator. Some need fulfillers are stronger reinforcers or punishers than others and provide a higher probability of motivation.

If too much time elapses between the presentation of the need fulfiller and the behavior, the need fulfiller may not serve as a reinforcer. The schedules by which the need fulfillers are provided make a difference in whether motivation is developed and maintained. There are some need fulfillers that the manager can provide, and there are others that are either unethical to provide or such that he has no control over them.

Reinforcers, punishers, and related means of motivating people are not new. They have always been and are still used in everyday life. The key here is for the manager to hone his motivational skills. But the author's intent is not to deal with the specifics of motivation, but rather to provide a general context. If a manager chooses to become familiar with the specifics, he can use any modern text in behavioral psychology.

The problem in management is not to understand behavioral principles and motivation, but to do something about it. Motivation should be developed with common sense. Constant demands or pressure and severe punishment can often decrease motivation, and it is important to know how much an individual can tolerate. Certainly, some pressure serves as a motivator and everyone needs a degree of it, including the manager.

Sometimes managers cannot identify things that fulfill needs. For example, one staff member might do anything to get mornings off to go duck hunting, whereas another might work overtime to write a center publication with his or her name on it. One staff member might feel punished if a manager does not take time to say hello and visit each morning; another might feel punished if he does not have a large office with a window. Sometimes the job itself is a need fulfiller. If it is not, perhaps it can be modified so it is.

Regulations within a job can often motivate individuals in certain ways. If a janitor is required to take care of all maintenance that a manager directs him to and is paid a set salary, he may act one way. But if the janitor is not paid a salary and if a manager is given a budget that he can use either to purchase services from the janitor or to purchase outside services, both the manager and the janitor may act another way. Management can certainly develop and modify regulations that provide the optimum contingency link.

The key to motivation is individual need. An effective management control system will certainly make use of models, performance standards, needs assessment data, and income statements, but it will also use individual need as a means of motivating staff in order to mold and shape the system.

The Informal Management Control System

It is not unusual to go into a building and see offices being switched, nameplates being changed, and employees moving. Typically that signifies something called reorganization, a fearsome word in most organizations. It primarily comes about because an administrator or group of administrators wants to modify the balance of control. Sometimes it happens so often that buildings have been designed with partitions that can be moved to make offices fit the new table of organization. When partitions cannot be moved fast enough, a method called landscaping can be resorted to; it makes use of portable carpeted dividers about neck high with which the building design can be modified daily or hourly.

Perhaps it does not matter if subordinate staff are housed in impersonal little cells as long as top administrators can see the physical structure. It is ironic but true that reorganization often has nothing to do with changing the balance of control. The people who control the system are still there; they are just located in another physical space. A manager can devise numerous new plans and change physical locations without ever really affecting the balance of control.

In every organization or system an informal management control system is operational. It has its own (informal) table of organization, information system (the grapevine), and data collection system (a black book). It has its reinforcers and punishers, all of whom serve to motivate individuals. Leaders in the informal system are often experts at controlling others; and if the formal system does not find or develop a place for them or get rid of them, they can use their skills to control the system in a manner that is not congruent with the organization.

That organizations identify certain persons as responsible does not mean those persons control the organization. For example, it is usual to believe that a state mental health or retardation institution is run by the superintendent, but many a superintendent who has overlooked the power of a business manager, the head engineer, the director of nursing, or even the superintendent's secretary has paid the price. One superintendent recognized that it was time for a salty old director of nursing to change her ways in order to change the strict medical model in his institution to a medical-developmental model. No matter how he tried, by making speeches, planning with staff, conducting in-service training, or visiting the wards, the medical model stayed intact. He even removed the director of nursing from the administration building in the hope of isolating her. That was all to no avail; for the director of nursing was in control of every nurse on every ward, and she knew how to maintain that control. There was no doubt on the part of the nursing staff about who ran the institution!

Some managers have mastered the informal system so well that they do not even use the formal one unless it is absolutely necessary. Some standard vouchers are used; standard reports are maintained; or regular pay increments are given; but most of the control comes through the informal system. The manager usually knows the needs of subordinates or supervisors and uses those needs as the basis for achieving aims. However, although managers can become successful with it, that approach leaves much to be desired. The problem is that the informal approach is by and large an underground and favored operation. No one really quite knows what the other person or group is doing. There are usually no performance data that tell anyone what is happening; there is no overall goal congruence; and a number of employees are left to run the services as they see fit. That leads to insecurity, jealousy, and resentment.

If the informal management control system is allowed to become predominant, formal management will become laissez faire. The behavior and performance of the organization can easily be guided by the self-interests of the individual. Of course, if that occurs, both the direction and the performance of the organization can become uncertain.

Regardless of what management might do, however, the informal system will always be operational to some degree. Managers can and should tolerate it to some extent. In fact, it can be used to attain some things that cannot be attained through the formal system. But its use should be limited, and the manager should rely on the formal system as the mechanism for attaining that which must be accomplished.

The Formal Management Control System

This section will describe some of the components of a formal management control system. Although such a system is frequently the point of jest, it is not only necessary but critical. It must be used to (1) define true human need, (2) plan identifiable and measurable human service systems, (3) implement and operate the systems, (4) manage staff, and (5) improve the systems. It provides the blueprint that explains what individuals are to do and provides precise criteria by which they will be evaluated. It should provide direction not once, but continuously.

The management control system, like the human service system, must be flexible. It must be in an ever-changing state in which effective concepts, instruments, and techniques are integrated and ineffective ones are aborted. It must also be efficient; it cannot consist of overpaid and ineffective managers or costly gadgets. Individual needs of personnel must be recognized, and personnel should be put in the position that best meets their needs and the needs of the organization.

Input from individuals at all levels of management must be obtained and truly considered in order to improve the service system, whether it be for strategic planning or day-to-day operation. When the managerial hierarchy is developed, it must be on the basis of the number of staff members that a manager can control. Control of submanagers should result in control of other staff.

In essence, the formal management control system contains much of what has been described in the preceding chapters. It can be based on the principles that have been discussed, and many of the instruments and techniques for needs assessment and performance evaluation can be integrated in it. Even some aspects of the informal system can be integrated, or at least allowed to become a part of the formal system.

Formal Management Control Functions

Management control functions generally include needs assessment, planning, implementing, operating, evaluating, and improving, which are typically initiated in a cycle. The management control system is used to define service products, provide the service products over time, insure quality, quantity, and cost, and improve the service system. The management control system is a subsystem within the human service system, and its needs can be defined, its objectives stated, and its products specified, evaluated, and improved in the same way that the service system is improved.

Management information systems

Producing accurate data is one of the more important functions of the management control system. Data are the basis upon which the majority of other functions are planned, and they are the raw material used to produce management products on which decisions are based. It is, therefore, critical that the optimum mix of data be obtained. Essential to securing that mix are (1) the questions to be answered, (2) the method for retrieving the data, (3) the importance of retrieving the data, and (4) the cost of retrieving the data. Finally, the data will have to be collected, tabulated, manipulated, and integrated into a final document. Management information systems are used for that purpose, and they should provide the information needed to manage the system.

Data are often collected and processed by computer; but that is not always necessary, nor are there always funds for such purposes. Computers offer an important advantage in that they can accurately manipulate and retrieve large amounts of data. Some of the functions that an EDP or manual data processing system should include are listed here:

1. Program product and cost performance data for overall impact.
2. Program product and cost performance data for organizational objectives assigned to a particular group or department within the human service system.
3. Program product and cost performance data for each organizational objective or combination of objectives.
4. Performance data that reflect the individual

employee's product output and the cost of his output in accomplishing organizational objectives.

5. Performance data that specify the service products and the cost of the service products for individual clients.

6. Program product and cost performance data for various management levels within an organization and by geographic areas inside and outside the organization.

7. Combined program product performance and income statements.

8. Summaries of monthly expenditures in terms of amounts expended and amounts remaining in standard accounting categories—travel, salaries, supplies.

9. Checks and balances when the data indicate recording errors.

Staff often use excessive time required for performance evaluation as an excuse not to evaluate. If done efficiently, it should not take more than 8 to 11 percent of staff time to plan and set up the system, and 2 to 4 percent of staff time to record and manipulate data and enter them on the final evaluation form. The charge made by some human service employees that evaluation requires too much time is unfounded. Businesses typically spend a minimum of 30 percent of their time that way, and government has suggested 10 percent for human services. The return on this small investment of staff time should certainly be considered in relation to the time spent in indecision or in making poor decisions.

Figure 6-1 is an example of a daily billing sheet used by staff to record both product and cost data. In addition to identifying data, it includes columns for the names

Figure 6-I. Weekly data collection form.

EMPLOYEE NAME: Bill Gross	EMPLOYEE NO. 0 0 1	GRANT NO. 0 3 4 7 8	BILLING MONTH No. 0 3	BILLING WEEK No. 0 3

Measurable Objective	I.D.	Client Name	Client No.	No. Miles Traveled	No. People Contacted	Job Description	Product	M	T	W	T	F	S	S	Total
Develop client program plans	2.2.1	J. Anderson	2074			Standard	1	6							6
		B. Jones	1086			Standard	1		4						4
		L. Loyd	5092			Special tests	1			8					8
		C. Ross	5080			Standard	1				6				6
						Subtotal	4								24
Evaluate staff performance	7.3.3	A. Thomas	008			Standard	1					1			1
		B. Smith	007			Standard	1					.5			.5
		C. Brown	004			Standard + planning	1					2			2
						Subtotal	3								3.5
Write grant	10.1	D. Carter	701			Not complete		2	4	0	4	4.5			14.5
						Total	7	8	8	8	10	8			42

and numbers of various objectives, the clients' names and ID numbers, job descriptions and products, and hours worked. Each month data are retrieved from the forms and processed through the system in order to determine monthly performance. The data are then plotted and compared with performance standards.

Holding staff accountable

Holding staff accountable is another important function of the management control system. Some managers are not satisfied with subordinates' work, so they often look over their shoulders and take responsibility and authority away informally. That leads to resentment and lack of productivity. Then the administrator is not a manager, but an administrator with an expanded workload and a resentful subordinate.

Responsibility centers that contain product, cost, or revenue performance centers must be used to bring about accountability. If the management control system does not make use of the evaluation centers, there is no effective way to decentralize or maintain control. At some programmed time or in certain situations, individual data must be reviewed and compared to performance standards, decisions must be made, and action regarding individual performance must be taken.

Far too often human service managers are reluctant to make evaluations of staff. It is a dreaded task to tell someone he is not performing well, and frequently time is not taken to inform someone when he is performing at a high level. In any case, the manager's job is to hold staff accountable. Using objective data for evaluation is a highly effective procedure for the purpose. Managers must accept the fact that performance evaluation is a major portion of their job. If the organization is to meet its objectives and the needs of its consumers, high performance by staff is essential.

It is not wrong to include personal objectives and develop some time lines or performance standards as long as the personal objectives are in line with the organization's mission and products. For example, if upgrading personal cost accounting skills improves cost accounting, why not help the staff member improve those skills?

Data can also be used to inform tertiary consumers or to exhibit the accountability of the human service system to its consumers. The management control system should include data-based progress reports. In fact, such reports should be required in the same way that quarterly reports are required of banks or large corporations. The performance reports should be communicated clearly and simply so that the intended population will understand them.

Contingency Links and the Management Control System

"How do I get someone motivated and headed in the right direction?" Basically, the first five chapters of this book include tools and techniques that can be used to determine directions and get the person headed in the right one. Keeping the person going in the right direction and at a reasonable rate is something else. Managers must be concerned with motivation and the use of contingency links to motivate people.

If the problem were to motivate rats to press a bar, the process would be simple. All that would be needed is a cage with a self-feeder that would release a food pellet each time a bar was pressed. The rat could be deprived of food to increase its food need, and at that point it would be motivated to press the bar and continue to do so until its hunger was satiated.

Obviously, people are not rats; and although it is not feasible to set up a comprehensive motivation or reinforcement system in human services at this time, it would be possible to do so. A sophisticated system that would reinforce staff for performance when and where needed could be developed and implemented. Systems technology such as that discussed in preceding chapters would be well suited for the purpose. The idea is not new, and some researchers have done pilot work on developing it. It is interesting to note that such a system can be developed to fit normal patterns of life, and that it can be humanizing.

One effective way to motivate staff is to provide systematic feedback regarding performance. In human services there are typically a number of restraints that would eliminate the use of money as an immediate reinforcer. For example, it is unlikely that a psychologist working for the state would be paid a piece rate for each child he tested. Yet payment per test could be the very reinforcer that builds and maintains testing behavior. If payment could not be made, then the next best thing would be to provide feedback on how the quantity and quality of testing each day was related to his yearly increase in salary.

Engineers describe feedback in a more precise way than most of us in human services. A human service manager might say, "Give me some feedback on this report"; in other words, "Give me some random comments." An engineer might say, "Each time the camshaft turns, it lifts each valve .025 inch. This feedback from the crankshaft enables fuel to be taken in and exhaust out through the valves at the precise time."

In human services, if service products have been specified so that they can be evaluted as to quality and quantity, precise performance feedback can be provided. If a contingency link, such as percent of salary increase, is bonded to performance data, feedback can be in terms of expected pay increase for delivered performance. Such feedback can be provided hourly, daily, weekly, or monthly, depending on the resources available. Even if feedback were provided on a monthly basis, it would be far superior to typical feedback that is provided only yearly, and then not on the basis of precise performance criteria.

Performance Evaluation and Feedback Tools

If there were only two things that will cause a manager to have personnel problems, they would probably be salary increases and promotions. The reason is that the value that an individual puts on himself is usually unrelated to work performance. It is not unusual to hear, "I'm just as good as she is" or "The boss must have been crazy to promote that guy over me." If the human service manager has no objective performance data to justify his position—and he typically has none—he will have to succumb.

It is not unusual for a human service manager to start out by providing salary increases on the basis of how he perceives various staff members' work. It is also not unusual that the judgments are subjective. As a result, a smooth-talking staff member could be perceived as a high performer, whereas a productive member with low verbal ability might be perceived as a low performer. If salary increases are based on subjective input, the contingency link is poor and the best performers could easily be deprived of their just rewards. Once more the smooth talker would actually be reinforced for smooth talking, not performance, and could well increase his smooth-talking behavior. On the other hand, the hard worker might slack off on performance because performance was not reinforced. Should that be the case, the manager would be motivating employees in a way that would produce low organizational performance.

Human service managers, for reason of those possible troubles, often give up on using salary increases as a means of motivation. They give the whole staff the same "merit" increases. They make excuses or provide inaccurate information to cover up low organizational performance. The tragedy is that staff members consciously or unconsciously recognize what is going on and take advantage of it. They even condemn the manager for allowing it to happen.

A manager of a telephone company once said: "Before anyone fires me, there will be a lot of my staff who will go first." What he meant was that the phone company itself is evaluated on the basis of employee service. If phones are not working or are not installed and removed upon customers' request or if there are major system problems, his head is on the chopping block. He cannot perform all the services himself, and therefore he must manage his staff in such a way that quality services are provided. If staff members do not do their jobs, the resulting poor service will be a reflection on the company, which is the manager's responsibility. Overall poor service for long periods could cost the manager his job. If it required firing staff in order to maintain high-quality service, then the manager would not hesitate to take that action for his company's good as well as his own.

Because of poor contingency links, human service managers pay little attention to performance. The results are minimal accountability and low-quality, inefficient services. Clients obtain illegal welfare payments; children are subjected to inhumane conditions; adolescents never learn to read; and elderly people starve to death. Even when administrators are terminated for low performance, something that happens far too infrequently, they go to another organization and it is business as usual.

To manage performance in human services effectively, a human service manager must (1) be committed to managing performance, (2) collect and use objective data, (3) evaluate performance systematically, and (4) be willing to provide monetary increases or other reinforcers or terminate staff on the basis of performance. He cannot ignore any of those areas; for to do so would be to weaken the contingency link.

Enough about managing performance—what tools should be used? A manager does not need reams and reams of data; he needs a few simple forms. Figure 6-2 is an example of a six-month evalution form that is used to consolidate performance data and provide feedback about the contingency link. Examples of three types of objectives—service, management, and special—are provided, along with performance data and percentage of recommended pay increases.

Of the three types of objectives, service objectives are the central ones, directly related to providing services to clients or support to the organization. Manage-

Figure 6-2. Six month performance evaluation form.

Name: J. P. Freeman

Dates: 1-1-79 5-30-79

Recommendations

1. Salary increase: Overall 79.1% increase recommended
2. Other: Performance trend increasing; no changes recommended

Monthly Performance Standards	January		February		March		April		May		June		Average	
	#	%	#	%	#	%	#	%	#	%	#	%	#	%
Develop 20 client program plans per month at quality stated in service objective	10	50	15	75	20	100	15	75	25	125	10	50	15.8	50.0
Evaluate 4 staff per month at quality stated in management objective	3	75	4	100	4	100	4	100	2	50	4	100	3.5	87.5
Write a special grant for state aide									1	100			1.0	100.0
Overall average														79.1

ment objectives are required to manage staff services for which a person is responsible. Both service and management objectives are developed as a result of an overall plan. Special objectives are either imposed on or selected by the person and are usually beyond the planned scope of work. Special objectives are sometimes of short duration and difficult to evaluate; however, they relate to performance and should be evaluated.

Special objectives are usually the result of a manager who imposes an additional workload or an employee who chooses to add a workload for organizational and also personal reasons. If too many special objectives are added by the manager or the staff member, the planned workload will be reduced and planned performance jeopardized.

The six-month evaluation form is a simple tool, but it can be an effective one. It was developed to display monthly performance data and the related percent of pay increase as well as the composite total for the six-month period. Information on the form is incorporated into a formal written report every six months. The report, based almost totally on the data from the six-month evaluation form, is presented to the employees. At that time, salaries are increased accordingly. If performance is too low, the recommendation could be termination; and the six-month evaluation report would provide objective evidence of the poor performance. If performance is high, additional reinforcers can be used.

Basically the six-month performance evaluation form contains identifying data, a list of performance objectives on the left, and a record of performance and pay increase data on the right. Once planning has been completed and the quality and quantity of objectives have been specified, an abbreviated version of the objective is recorded on the evaluation form. Each month the performance data are recorded and compared with the performance standard in the objective. Then the percent of pay increase for the month is computed by determining the percent of variance from the standard, if any. Percentage, as with variance, could be below, at, or above 100 percent. For example, in the first objective, the performance standard was 20 client program plans per month. During the first month actual performance was 10, a variance of −10, or 50 percent of the standard. Therefore, the salary increase for that month would be 50 percent of the total available for the monthly increase. If $100 per month were available, the increase would be $50. Remember that the payment is not made each month, but at the end of six months. The final average for the total percentages over a six-month period is used to determine the actual raise. The $50 represents feedback from withholding the reinforcer; and five months are available for the employer to make up the difference.

Not all objectives are of equal weight. For example, client services might be of highest weight and management objectives of lesser weight. A special objective that is added because of a highly important situation could be considered to be of higher weight than the service or management objective, even if it occurred during a one-month period. At some point the weights and performance data could be used to determine salary increases. If a manager chose not to use the weighting system, he could use a straight percentage system. Both examples are provided in Figure 6-3. (In the salary computations, $600 is used as the standard bimonthly raise.)

Other methods can be used to determine the final average, but it is suggested that the manager not use complicated formulas. In the end, most of the objectives and their worth should balance out. Weights should be used only because performance needs to be increased or decreased in a certain area and requires special consideration.

One last word about collecting performance data: managers sometimes question the reliability of the data. Employees can fake data to gain the higher percent of the salary. There will, of course, always be some data unreliability even when good records are kept. The manager can tolerate a certain amount of error because the cost of gaining precise accuracy would be hard to justify. When high unreliability is suspected, however, audits can be used to check the data and the manager may choose to spot-check the quality and quantity of services. Ideally, spot checks and audits should be applied frequently through a variable ratio schedule.

Finally, who manages the manager? If there is no one who chooses to evaluate the manager's performance, the "buck stops there." The manager must evaluate his own

Figure 6-3. Two methods of computing salary increases using performance data.

	Straight Percentage		Weighting			
	#	%	#	%	Wt.	Tot.
Objective 1	15.8	50.0	15.8	50.0	3	150
Objective 2	3.5	87.5	3.5	87.5	2	175
Objective 3	1.0	100.0	1.0	100.0	4	400
Total		237.5				725
Average	237.5 ÷ 3	79.1	900 = 100%		725 = 87%	
Salary	.791 x $600 = $475		.87 x $600 = $522			

performance, and that can be dangerous. A manager can find himself not motivated to plan management objectives, much less evaluate them. Because management objectives are directly concerned with performance of staff, overall organization performance will certainly deteriorate and may even disappear if they are not met. The manager must set up his own evaluation and become conditioned to using it.

Conclusion

In the final analysis, everyone is a manager. The commissioner of the human development division manages the superintendent, who manages the director of nursing, who manages a staff member, who manages a client, who manages another client. Management is a way of life. Every day there are numerous instances in which we are managers or are required to manage others. The job can be drab, lonesome, or boring, or it can be colorful, stimulating, and exciting. It depends upon what a manager wants to make it and what instruments and techniques he uses.

Management is coming into its own as a profession. People who choose to become leaders should be trained to lead as they are trained in their special fields. If staff members are promoted to management positions, they should be trained in management. Universities should teach some management courses to all students and continually update courses offered for administrators. Courses in plant and physical facilities should be supplemented with systems analysis and design courses. Statistical courses should include functional approaches for evaluating performance, and methods courses should certainly include staff needs assessment, consumer needs assessment, and motivation.

Where do we go from here? It is hoped that this book has provided some useful information that will fit the reader's individual management model. If this material is combined with other information to improve human services for the consumer, we will all share the rewards.

Bibliography

Anthony, R. N., *Management Accounting Principles*. Homewood, Ill.: Irwin, 1970.

Banghart, F. W., *Educational Systems Analysis*. New York: Macmillan, 1969.

Blatt, B., and F. Kaplan, *Christmas in Purgatory*. Boston: Allyn & Bacon, 1974.

Budde, J. F., *Analyzing and Measuring Deinstitutionalization across Residential Environments with Alternative Living Environments Rating and Tracking System (ALERT)*, A Publication of KUAF at the University of Kansas, Lawrence, Kansas, 1976.

Budde, J. F., *Formative Management of Human Service*, A Publication of KUAF at the University of Kansas, Lawrence, Kansas, 1976.

Budde, J. F., and M. E. Edwards, *Statewide Planning: Least-Restrictive Residential Services*, A Publication of KUAF at the University of Kansas, Lawrence, Kansas, 1978.

Churchman, C. W., *Systems Approach*. New York: Delta, 1969.

Davis, R. H., and R. Behan, "Evaluating Systems Performance in Simulated Environments," in R. M. Gagne (ed.), *Psychological Principles in Systems Development*. New York: Holt, Rinehart and Winston, 1962

Donaldson v. *O'Connor*, Florida 493 F. 2d 507 (5th Cin. 1974).

Drucker, P. F., *Management: Tasks, Responsibilities, Practices.* New York: Harper & Row, 1974

Establishing the Legal Rights of Mentally Retarded Citizens. *In Compendium of Law Suits* (PCMR/DHEW Publication No. COHD 75–21007). Washington, D.C.: GPO, 1974.

Etz, D. V., "The First Management Consultant?" *Management Review,* 1964, vol. 53, pp. 54–57.

Getzels, J. W., "Administration as a Social Process," in A. W. Halpin (ed.), *Administrative Theory in Education.* Chicago: University of Chicago, 1958.

Herzberg, F., *Work and the Nature of Man.* Cleveland: World, 1966.

Maslow, A. H., *Motivation and Personality.* New York: Harper & Row, 1954.

Pennypacker, H. S., Keonig, H. C., and Lindsley, O. R., *Handbook of the Standard Behavior Chart.* Gainesville, Fla.: Pennypacker, 1972.

Public Law 94–103, 94th Congress HR4005, Oct. 4, 1975 (89 Stat. 486 59–674 (122) 0–75).

Silverman, L. C., *Systems Engineering of Education V: Quantitative Concepts for Education Systems.* Los Angeles: Education & Training Consultants, 1972.

Smith, B. C., "Process Control: A Guide to Planning," in P. Davidson (ed.), *Evaluation of Behavioral Programs in Community, Residential, and School Settings: Proceedings Banff International Conference on Behavior.* Champaign, Ill.: Research Press, 1974.

Stufflebeam, D., *Educational Evaluation and Decision Making.* Itasca, Ill.: Peacock, 1971.

Tarkenton, F., "The Keys to Motivation," *Sky,* 1978, vol. 1, no. 11, pp. 8–12.

Wolfensberger, W., and L. Glenn, *Pass III.* New York: National Institute on Mental Retardation, 1975.

Index